COUNTRY SCRAP-BOOK

for

BOYS and GIRLS

By MALCOLM SAVILLE

First published 1944
Second (enlarged) Edition 1945

Gramol Publications, Ltd.
London and Chesham.

Acknowledgments

I am indebted to the following authors, authors' representatives and publishers for permission to reprint material of which they control the copyright :

To Mrs. Frances Cornford for her poem *Spring Morning*.

To the Executors of the late W. H. Davies and Messrs. Jonathan Cape, Limited, for the poem *Leisure* from " Collected Poems by W. H. Davies."

To the Society of Authors as literary representatives of the Trustees of the late A. E. Housman and Messrs. Jonathan Cape, Limited, publishers of A. E. Housman's " Collected Poems," for the poem *Loveliest of trees, the Cherry now*.

To Mrs. George Bambridge for *Puck's Song* from " Puck of Pook's Hill," by the late Rudyard Kipling, published by Macmillan and Company, Limited.

To Messrs. G. Bell and Sons, Limited, for permission to reprint the poem *The Year* by Coventry Patmore.

To the author, Dorothy Una Ratcliffe, and Messrs. John Lane the Bodley Head, Limited, for three poems, *The City Child*, *February* and *The Spring*.

To Messrs. Macmillan and Company, Limited, and the author's representative, for permission to reprint Christina Rossetti's poem *Winter*.

To Mr. Lloyd Osbourne, for permission to reprint the three poems by Robert Louis Stevenson, *Farewell to the Farm*, *Summer Sun* and *The Cow*.

To Mr. A. G. Street for the extract *Groveley Wood in March*, from the author's " A Country Calendar," published by Messrs. Eyre and Spottiswoode (Publishers), Limited.

To Messrs. Jonathan Cape, Limited, for the poem *Green Rain* from " Poems and The Spring of Joy," by the late Mary Webb.

To Mr. Clarence Winchester for his poem *Winter has Departed* from " Earthquake in Los Angeles and Other Poems," published by Messrs. Cassell and Company, Limited.

2

Contents

Illustrations

Photographs by British Council, G. Denes, Eric J. Hosking, Germaine Kanova, Technical and Industrial Press Service, Nancy Sandys Walker.

Drawings on jacket by C. F. Tunnicliffe.

Photographs on end papers : British Council.

If you are interested in printing, you may like to know that the coloured paper dust jacket of this book is printed " letterpress " from four line copper plates, one for black and one each for the three colour printings. The " end papers " are printed " offset " from prepared metal plates which offset an ink impression which is then transferred by contact to the paper from a rubber surface. The text of the book is printed letterpress from type cast by a Monotype machine. You should see how this is done if you ever visit a printing works. The photographic illustrations on the art-paper sections are printed letterpress from half-tone copper plates—look at the pictures through a strong magnifying-glass and you will see the dots of the half-tone screen which enable the pictures to be printed clearly.

Foreword

IT may seem strange to tell you at the beginning of a book about the country and wild life that England is yours and that when you are grown-up you will have to look after her. But this is so, because England is one of those countries where the people who live in it have a share in its planning and government.

I am sure you know, too, that there is no country in the world for which so many sacrifices have been made and which holds so many treasures. It is probably difficult for you to remember that before the war it was possible to have holidays at the seaside or on a farm and to draw the curtains wide at night. And because of the war you may never have had a chance to see our own countryside, which is the loveliest and rarest of Britain's treasures.

This book is to help you to enjoy all the wonderful things which the country has to offer and to understand what life in the country really means. People from all over the world have always come to Britain to see what we are often too busy, too lazy or indifferent to discover for ourselves. They come to see our cathedrals, our little market towns, our rolling English roads and the village churches built with the loving hands of craftsmen of a bygone age. They stand in wonder at the sight of the Scottish lakes and glens, of majestic Snowdon or Cader Idris, or at the green, windswept solitude of the Downs that run down to the southern sea.

All these places are your heritage. They are the Britain for which so many of her sons have fought and died. One day the countryside will pass into your keeping to guard and

5

cherish in your turn, and it is important to remember that it is very easily spoiled.

It is often difficult to love and respect something which we do not know very well, and so I hope that this book will send you adventuring out into the fields, forests and hillsides of our own land, to explore and discover for yourself the unchanging spirit of England, which is not so easy to recognise when it is hidden by bricks and mortar.

Although I have tried to tell you enough about the country to make you want to see more of it for yourself, it seemed to me to be a good idea to show you, at the same time, some of the splendid and beautiful words which have been written by English men and women about the country they loved above all others. You will also find some suggestions for other books to read about the country and wild life—books which are very much more learned and clever than this one, and I hope these will give you in more detail what I am often only able to suggest, here.

Do not think that the country is dull because there is not a cinema at the corner of every winding lane. There is more to do in the country than in the town ; more to see and more to learn and remember. The country does not exist merely for the pleasure of those who live in the towns. The country was there first, but you will not enjoy it as you should unless you know what to look for and how to treat it.

And so before you come adventuring into the country with me, read the lovely lines printed opposite, written by one whose great love of birds, animals and nature has given us many beautiful poems. He knew, as so many of us still have to learn, that we miss the best in life if we travel too fast to see the beauty around us.

M. S.

WESTEND FARM,
WHEATHAMPSTEAD.

LEISURE

What is this life if, full of care,
We have no time to stand and stare?

No time to stand beneath the boughs
And stare as long as sheep and cows.

No time to see, when woods we pass,
Where squirrels hide their nuts in grass.

No time to see, in broad daylight,
Streams full of stars, like skies at night.

No time to turn at Beauty's glance,
And watch her feet, how they can dance.

No time to wait till her mouth can
Enrich that smile her eyes began.

A poor life this if, full of care,
We have no time to stand and stare.

W. H. DAVIES

A ripple of land ; such little hills, the sky
Can stoop to tenderly and the wheatfields climb ;
Such nooks of valleys lined with orchises,
Fed full of noises by invisible streams ;
And open pastures where you scarcely tell
White daisies from white dew,—at intervals
The mythic oaks and elm-trees standing out
Self-poised upon their prodigy of shade,—
I thought my father's land was worthy too
Of being my Shakespeare's.

  . . . .

The happy violets hiding from the roads
The primroses run down to, carrying gold ;
The tangled hedgerows, where the cows push out
Impatient horns and tolerant churning mouths
'Twixt dripping ash-boughs,—hedgerows all alive
With birds and gnats and large white butterflies
Which look as if the May-flower had caught life
And palpitated forth upon the wind ;
Hills, vales, woods, netted in a silver mist,
Farms, granges, doubled up among the hills ;
And cattle grazing in the watered vales,
And cottage-chimneys smoking from the woods,
And cottage-gardens smelling everywhere,
Confused with smell of orchards.

       ELIZABETH BARRETT BROWNING

The Farm

W HEN we go into the country for a holiday, or perhaps only
for a day, we generally think of a farm. To many of us the
country means a farm, and it is difficult to realise that anything else happens away from the towns except farming.
And, of course, this is really true, for farming is the industry
of the countryside and was indeed the first work of the first
men who lived in our country. You have probably heard
about the people who lived many thousands of years ago in
caves and who clothed themselves in skins and had to hunt
wild animals to live. After a time, man began to tame some
of the animals he had been hunting, and most people believe
that he tamed the dog first to help him hunt and round up
the wild cattle, horses, sheep and goats. (There is a very
good story of how the dog and other animals came to work
for men, called " The Cat that Walked by Himself " in
Rudyard Kipling's *Just So Stories*.)

We suppose it was about the same time that he found
the seeds of some plants could be eaten, and so he began
to cultivate wheat and other cereal crops and store food for
the winter.

This is how farming began, and although to-day in some
of the great wheat-growing countries like the Middle West
of the United States or Canada or Australia, or grazing
countries like the Argentine, the farms are so big that it
would take you many, many days to walk round them, here
in our own land the farms are small and no two of them are
alike, and the buildings, the fields and the crops vary with the
soil and the type of country in which they are set. A farm
in Lincolnshire, for instance, where the soil is rich and dark,
is quite different from a farm in Sussex, where the soil is
chalky. But whatever differences we should see if we travelled
up and down our country, farming still remains our oldest
industry. There were farms before there were villages, and

there is no place more typical of our country and all our characteristics than a farm. And that is why we start our book about the country by telling you some of the things you will see on a farm.

* * *

"DON'TS" ON THE FARM

Most people who live in towns seem to think that the farmer and the men who work for him are slow, and if not actually lazy, certainly do not work very hard. Perhaps this silly idea has grown up because the countryman knows that you cannot hurry nature and that work which is rushed is never good work. Animals hate being hurried. A field carelessly ploughed grows a poor crop ; a ditch only half cleaned soon gets choked again, and a hastily thatched rick will fall to pieces in the first winter gale. Every season has its special tasks and every day the farmer has a dozen problems, while a sudden change in the weather can unsettle all the plans he has made.

So remember, when you do pay your visit to a farm, that the farmer, even if he doesn't look it, is a very busy man. You can be certain that he is up before six o'clock every morning of his life and that his day's work out of doors does not finish until the light has gone. He probably works harder than any other man you know, and when you have made a friend of him you will understand why a farmyard must not be treated as a playground.

Here are some of the things you must *not* do when you are a guest or a visitor to a farm.

You must never leave gates open. If the gate to a field is shut, be careful to close it behind you and to latch it firmly. Serious damage can be done by straying cattle, and it really is important to remember that if a gate was closed when you came to it, it was shut for a very good reason.

Neither must you break down hedges or fences at blackberrying time or holly-cutting time. If you see a hole in the hedge, don't make it bigger by crawling through it.

And you must not play in the water troughs or drop anything in the water, because it is easy to pollute the water and poison a valuable horse or cow.

Neither must you slide down haystacks nor play with fire in any way near the ricks or barns. Your friend the farmer will remain your friend if you do not scramble over or play with his tractors or other implements which he keeps under cover somewhere in the farmyard.

For your own sake, do not come up behind a farm horse when he is drinking or in his stall and pat him unexpectedly before he has seen you. He does not like being surprised, and may kick.

Be careful, please, not to leave broken glass where it can injure any of the stock—animals on a farm are referred to as stock, livestock.

It is wiser not to go into any of the milking-sheds without permission, because these have to be kept scrupulously clean.

Although all this sounds as if you won't be able to go anywhere or do anything, it really is only a matter of courtesy. If you try to remember that it is as if a stranger came into your house and, without being invited, opened the doors and windows, jumped on the furniture and broke it and interfered with whatever your mother was doing, then you will see the farmer's point of view. Most farmers will be glad to let you go anywhere and see everything if you ask them first, and show them that you know how to behave.

* * *

CATTLE

On most farms in the British Isles you will find some cattle, by which we mean cows and bulls and their kind. Some herds of cattle are kept for us to eat in the form of beef and some are kept for milking. You may think that all cows are alike and that they are a rather frightening sort of animal as they raise their heads to stare at you when you hurry along the field path. There are many different breeds of cattle in these islands, and it is rather fun if you can learn to recognise some of them. First of all, though, it is important to remember the names given to male and female cattle. You know, of course, that a cow's baby is a calf and it remains a calf until it is a year old, when it is called a stirk. Then, if it is a male which is to be kept for breeding, it becomes a bull. A heifer is the name for the female stirk, and she is called a heifer until she has had her second calf, when she becomes a cow. It all sounds rather complicated, but your farmer friend will think a lot more of you if you know the difference between a heifer and a cow.

The most common breed of cattle in our islands is the Shorthorn, and though you will see her more in the north than the south, she is a fairly big animal and is easy to recognise anywhere with her shortish, curly horns and red, roan or white colouring.

Another fine-looking breed is the Hereford, which is most seen in the Midland counties and North Wales. Herefords are large, deep red in colour, with long horns, but what makes them so easy to remember is the white face and chest. They have been exported to such countries as North and South America and Australia, where cattle wander over the immense grazing ranges. When you next see a " Western " film, where the cowboys are rounding up cattle, look carefully and you will probably see that the stampeding cows have white faces and chests. Herefords are bred mainly for beef and are extremely strong and hardy.

Another breed which made friends in other parts of the world is the Red Poll. Originally these big red animals came from Norfolk and Suffolk, but now they have gone to Australia and New Zealand, and are particularly hardy and useful, because they are bred for both beef and milking. Cattle without horns are always called " polled," so the Red Poll is easy enough to recognise without her horns.

Probably the one breed you would be certain to know is the Jersey—a small and really beautiful-looking animal of soft fawn colour. As the name suggests, Jerseys come from the Channel Islands, where the original breed was even smaller than the descendants here and overseas. The Jersey has the look of a deer about her, and for her size no cow gives as much rich milk.

A similar breed is the Guernsey, which is larger than the Jersey, and her milk is even richer, and you may remember that many dairy companies used to advertise a Guernsey Herd.

I've told you almost enough about cattle, because you are only likely to see one single breed on any one farm. But I must remind you of the Friesian, which is a big black and white animal which came originally from Holland. You will see her in all parts of the country, and no other cow can equal her milk yield.

Now you can see that there really is a difference between the various breeds of cattle, and what I've told you here is easy enough to remember. At the farm be sure to ask if you can see the cows being milked. It's fun to see them coming in from pasture and taking their places patiently at their stalls. Notice how spotlessly clean the milking-shed is kept, and how the milker seats himself with his head against the cow's side, and how the milk spurts into the pail. Milking is done mechanically on some farms, but this is not general.

Because I always think of the cow as a particularly friendly kind of animal, in spite of her size and the way she stares at you, I like what Robert Louis Stevenson wrote about her.

THE COW

The friendly cow, all red and white,
*   I love with all my heart:*
She gives me cream with all her might,
*   To eat with apple tart.*

She wanders lowing here and there,
*   And yet she cannot stray,*
All in the pleasant open air,
*   The pleasant light of day;*

And blown by all the winds that pass,
*   And wet with all the showers,*
She walks among the meadow grass
*   And eats the meadow flowers.*

ROBERT LOUIS STEVENSON

HORSES

Even now, when so much farm work is done by tractors, it would be difficult to find a farm without horses. Right from the earliest times the horse has been the gentle and willing servant of man, and for certain work no machinery can take his place. If you have never seen a pair of horses coming up over the brow of a hill and drawing the plough steadily behind them, you have missed a thrilling sight. Quietly and without fuss the great sure-footed beasts seem to know the ploughman's will and each other's habits so that they stop and turn and pull again with wonderful intelligence. Sometimes you will see farm horses harnessed to the big wheeled carts hauling in the root crops, and then, if the weather is bad, you will realise that the horse can haul a cart over muddy fields and rough tracks when the tractor would sink or stick in the mud.

You ought to know the names which a farmer calls his horse at various stages of its life. A baby horse is a foal (if your visit to the farm is in the spring, you should ask whether any foals have been born yet, as they are, I think, the most fascinating of all baby animals). A foal is a filly foal if she is female, or a colt foal if male. When a filly is old enough to be mated she becomes a mare, and the colt is called a stallion.

There are many different breeds of horses, but not many farmers now keep a horse to pull a trap to market, because they go by car. The horses you are most likely to see about the farm are the " work-horses "—great big fellows with long hair growing on the lower back parts of their legs. Of these there are three famous breeds—the Shire, the Clydesdale and the Suffolk Punch. The Shire is the biggest and strongest horse in the world. He is a beautiful animal and very gentle and good-tempered and most intelligent. The Clydesdale is not quite so heavy as the Shire, but generally taller, and you are more likely to meet him in the Northern counties. He generally has more white about his legs than the Shire. The Suffolk Punch, as his name suggests, came first from East

Anglia, and he is still to be found there more than anywhere else. He is not as large as the other two breeds, but almost as strong, very long-lived and clean-legged.

You may be curious to know how long a work-horse lives, and the answer is between twenty and thirty years, but these big horses are not fit for much heavy work after twenty.

Another thing that may have puzzled you about the horse is the phrase that his size is " so many hands." A horse is not measured in inches in the usual way, although a " hand " is four inches, which is about the width of a man's hand. His height is measured from the top of his shoulders to the ground.

If you become as fond of horses as most children, you will never tire of watching them at work or munching contentedly in their stable. And if you are ever lucky enough to be on the farm in the early days of May—with some farmers it is always the first of May—when the work-horses are released from their stables and put out to grass, you will see something you will never forget. The big fellows go almost wild with delight as they thunder crazily round the field, flinging up their great hooves, tossing their mighty heads and shaking their manes in joy and excitement at feeling soft grass under their feet again.

* * *

SHEEP

I always think the most interesting thing about sheep is that lambs are born early in the year at a time when winter is only half-way gone and spring a distant dream. In some parts of our country—particularly in the south, where it is not so cold—a few lambs are born before Christmas; but if you are on a farm where there are sheep during January, February and March, you will find that the shepherd has little rest during those months. Up in the mountains of Scotland, where the grass comes late, lambs are not born until May.

It is difficult to believe that there are more sheep in this country than any other of man's animals, but this is so. There are very many different breeds of British sheep, and I don't think it is necessary to know the names of them. It is interesting, however, to realise that they vary in size and appearance with their district, and when you are able to travel about the country you will soon see the difference in a day's journey by car or train.

If you started your journey in that fascinating and lonely part of Kent called Romney Marsh, you would find sheep everywhere—a big close-wooled sheep with a white face and a black nose. He has been bred here for years, and although he has been exported all over the world, he won't be found very far from his native air in England. If we continued our journey to the west and climbed up from the levels of the land which once was covered by the sea to Hastings, and then made for the chalk hills that run into the sea at East-bourne, we should find another and a most famous breed dotting every fold and sweep of the Downs. The Southdown is a small, dark-faced breed, and is another which has been sent to all parts of the world.

In Devon we should find a long-wooled type and yet another sort on Dartmoor. On the Welsh hill-tops another hardy little chap is different again from anything we have yet seen, and so, when you came to the borderlands and Shropshire and across to Yorkshire and up to the hills of Cumberland, you would find differing types. Some are bred solely for mutton and some grow long wool and some short, but because in some ways the sheep is the least domesticated of the animals man has tamed for his own use and is always out of doors in all weathers, you will not see any about the farm buildings. But lambs, at the turn of the year, are always a joy to see, as they are a promise of spring, and it has always been a wonder to me that such an engaging and amusing baby animal as a lamb can grow into such a stupid and uninteresting animal as a sheep! Perhaps you won't agree with this—certainly no shepherd would.

The names shepherds call their sheep at different stages of their life vary very much in different parts of the country, but you should know that a female lamb is called a ewe lamb and the male a ram or tup. Lambs are weaned

Maybe he's going to market, but it doesn't look as if he likes the idea of leaving his mother

Cows
coming
in
to be
milked.

*A fine pedigree bull ; he is worth a lot of
money to his owner.*

Fruits of the harvest ; threshing.

The farm's most patient workers.

" Reynard the Fox " helps to keep down rabbits and rats—the farmer's enemies—but kills poultry and lambs as well.

" Brock the Badger " ; a shy, plucky and fascinating animal.

from their mother at about five months and are then called hoggs (note that this sort of hogg has two g's). Of course male or female is called tup hogg or ewe hogg. They continue to be known as hoggs until their first shearing at about fourteen to sixteen months old, and when they are mated a few months later they are known as ewes and tups or rams respectively.

But you will find out more about sheep in ten minutes by talking to a shepherd than any book can tell you.

*　　　*　　　*

PIGS

Since the outbreak of war there have not been nearly so many pigs kept in this country, but your farm may be one of those with an old-fashioned brick-built sty containing seven or eight squealing piglets and an enormous sow. Some people find the pig a friendly and engaging animal, and certainly the sow is a good mother.

Pigs really need more artificial conditions than any other farm animals. You will realise that they are not left free to wander over the fields but are given comparatively little space and that they fatten quickly and breed easily under these conditions. There are not nearly so many breeds of British pigs as there are of sheep.

Pigs are destructive animals and remarkably strong. They will burrow with their snouts under fences and hedges, and that is why you will sometimes see them with rings through their sensitive noses. A stubborn pig will soon see reason when the drover slips his stick through the ring to lead him to market !

The names of pigs are easy to remember. The mother pig is a sow and the father a boar. The babies are called piglets or piglings and are called weaners when they are weaned at about ten weeks old. A female weaner is called a gelt until she has had her second litter and then she becomes a sow.

Pigs love being tickled and will grunt with pleasure if you rub their backs hard with a stick. There's no need for you to know the names of all the different breeds, but you can easily remember that the standard bacon pig in this country and in Denmark, Canada and the United States is the Large White. And he looks exactly like that! There is also a Large Black and a Middle White—the latter a rather repulsive-looking animal with a *very* upturned snout.

* * *

THE FARMHOUSE

Now that we have had a look at the animals you will find on or around the farm, let us explore the farm buildings and the farmhouse before we go out into the fields to see what is growing.

Somehow a modern farmhouse never looks or seems to be as exciting as an old one, and most of the farmhouses in these islands are very old. Nearly always they blend happily with the country in which they are set, because they have been made of local materials, and usually stand on a site where man has farmed in one way or another for hundreds of years. Look for yourself and you will soon realise how cunningly the early farmers placed their first buildings— sometimes in the valley, sometimes in a fold of the hills so that they are sheltered from the prevailing winds, and always where there is water. You will see how the trees have generally been set to act as a weather break and often— particularly in the south and west where the gales come roaring in from the Atlantic—the branches of the trees have been bent by the force of the wind until they seem to be growing with it.

The kitchen is the heart of the farmhouse. Of course we all know that the kitchen is where the work is done in *every* house—but somehow in the farmhouse it seems more important still, because it is nearly always the living-room as well as where the cooking is done.

When Mrs. Farmer asks you in, look first for the big oak dressers and the enormous kitchen range where a fire burns summer and winter alike. Even in England to-day many farmsteads are without gas or electricity, so you may see an oil lamp hanging from the black-beamed ceiling. The floor may be flagged with stone, and quite likely a row of brass and copper preserving pans and saucepans will wink at you from a high shelf or mantelpiece, and there will almost certainly be a big grandfather clock ticking solemnly in the corner. Everybody uses the kitchen, and you will feel at once that it is the room round which everything else in the house revolves.

Big, cool larders and the dairy with its stone shelves may lead out of the kitchen, as may the back door. You will soon find that nobody seems to use the front door, and I suppose this is because those living in the house come to it through the farmyard with dirt all over their boots.

*   *   *

THE FARMYARD

Farm buildings and farmyards are full of surprises. The stable you have found already, but the great barns are always worth exploring. At certain times of the year they will be almost bursting with the stores of golden grain—yellow, shining corn that slips through your fingers in a glittering stream—waiting for the miller to collect. Potatoes, too, may be kept this way under cover, although if the fields are far from the farm, the potatoes may be stored where they were harvested, in " clamps," under a protective covering of soil and straw. Sometimes the farmers have to use their barns for storing sacks of artificial manure, and often in a corner you will find the cutting machine which shreds up the swedes and mangolds for the cattle in the winter months when they cannot be put out to grass.

Under cover you will also find the carts and waggons and the more exciting tractors, ploughs, disc-harrows and automatic sowers and combine harvesters, and in another part of the farmyard will be found the water troughs for the horses and cattle. Many farms in remote districts are without water laid on, and must rely upon wells and a pump. Not until you have lived in a house without an endless supply of water can you realise how precious it is and how, in dry seasons, the farmer anxiously watches the depth of water in his well.

Then there are cowsheds—sometimes called byres— where the cattle are sheltered in the winter when there is no fresh grass for them in the fields. You will see how busy the dairy farmer is likely to be during these dark months, because cows eat a great deal of food—hay and chopped roots, such as swedes and mangolds—and they must be kept clean, too, and bedded down with clean straw. The byre may have to be cleaned out several times a day, and all soiled straw and dung will be shifted out on to the great steaming heap of manure, which will be ploughed into the fields in the spring. So valuable is this manure that nearly every farmer—even if he does not reckon to be a dairy farmer—keeps some cattle for this very purpose of converting straw into farmyard manure which is essential for enriching the soil.

*　　　*　　　*

THE STACKYARD

The one part of the farm we have not noticed yet is the stackyard, which is generally next to the farmyard. In the summer when it is little more than a patch of rough grass marked with irregular rectangles where last season's stacks stood, you may well wonder why this ground is being wasted. But in the winter it is a very different sight, when the great golden stacks stand firm against the weather waiting for the thresher to come and, in a cloud of dust and chopped straw, send the grain pouring into the waiting sacks.

But you should really see the stackyard at harvest-time on a lovely summer's evening in August, when the ricks are being built, and see how the farmhand stands on the top of the cart, tosses up the sheaves on a pitchfork to his mate, who catches them in the same way and builds up the rick around himself until at last he is nine or ten feet from the ground. Some days later when the rick has " settled " the thatcher comes and finishes off the job by giving the rick a roof of straw which will keep out the rains and winds of winter. Thatching is very skilled work, and in some parts of the country a good thatcher goes from farm to farm in the season, hiring himself out to the farmers who are impatiently waiting to have their harvest made safe before the weather breaks.

Generally it is months later before the farmer is ready for the threshing machine. On big corn-growing farms he probably has his own thresher, but on smaller farms he must hire a machine and wait his turn as the thresher tours the countryside.

It is great fun to watch the thresher at work, and threshing day is one of the most exciting on the farm. Work generally starts very early, and although the machine is worked by a tractor or steam traction engine, eight to ten men are needed to tend it. A normal thresher can thresh between 150 to 200 sacks of grain a day.

The sheaves from the ricks are thrown on to the endless band of the elevator which carries them to the top of the machine. Inside, the grain is knocked out of the straw by a fast-revolving drum and, after passing through various shaking sieves which remove from it seeds of weeds and dust, pours out into the sacks ready to receive it below. Meanwhile the chaff is blown away and the straw is either trussed or chopped and delivered at the other end. Some machines blow the chopped straw out of big tubes like a chimney.

As each stack is finished the men pick up sticks and cudgels and call the dogs for a rat hunt, for rats are among the farmers' greatest enemies, and they nest underneath the stacks.

At the end of the day, when the thresher has finished its work, the stackyard looks very messy and untidy, but the straw will all be used again for the cattle, and will, in time, go back again into the earth from which it sprang.

* * *

THE FIELDS

The crops you see growing in the fields round the farm will vary as the soils in different parts of the country vary. Light, sandy soil does not hold water well and is not suitable for wheat, but barley can be grown on it. If you ever go to

Lincolnshire, where much of the land has been reclaimed, you will see that the soil is black and rich, and potatoes thrive on this. Wheat likes a heavier soil, as do beans, so you must not expect to see the same sort of crops growing on every farm.

Some fields on every farm will be kept for hay, and although most of these were relentlessly ploughed up during the war, the farmer must have some hay on which to feed his stock in the winter.

There are four types of cereals grown in this country—wheat, oats, barley and rye. Wheat is our biggest crop, of course, and some types are sown in the autumn and, if the winter is mild, you can see the fields tinged with the blue-green of new growth at Christmas. Spring wheat is sown in February, oats in March and barley not until April.

After the fields have been ploughed—some in the autumn and some in the spring, according to the crop to be sown—the ridges are broken up with the harrow so that the soil is made fine and fit for the tiny seeds. Sowing is done by a machine drawn by a horse or tractor, which automatically makes ten or more evenly spaced drills and drops the seed into them from the container above. The harrow follows the sower to cover up the seeds and keep them from the thieving birds, and then comes the roller. The roller is used again to firm the soil after the wheat is up.

So on your farm you may find fields of wheat and oats, but you are not likely to find a farm growing all four cereals. Rye is not grown much in the south. Potatoes you are almost certain to find. These are set or sown in the spring in ridges and the ground must be well manured first. They are harvested in September or October by an ingenious machine with revolving forks which breaks down the ridges and throws the potatoes up to the surface.

Other root crops you may find are carrots, which are easily recognisable, with their feathery green leaf, and sugar beet, with its heavy, fleshy leaf. Turnips, swedes and mangolds are all valuable, and the farmer must grow some roots for his cattle to eat in the winter. Crops like these need much more work than the cereals because the fields must be weeded at least three times during the summer. The seedlings must be thinned also, and this is a back-breaking job which must be done by hand. Down the long rows the farmer's men—sometimes this work is done by women—must go with their hoes pulling out the young plants so that there is a three- or four-inch space between each. Sometimes a horse-hoe has been down the rows first, loosening the soil a few inches below the surface so that the weeds are uprooted and die. After the hand-hoeing it is sometimes necessary to thin still further by hand, because plants—and particularly big root crops like swedes—must have room to grow.

Sometimes in the early summer when you are walking in the country and the wind is blowing towards you, it may bring to you a sickly, sweet smell, and you will know that you are near a field of beans in flower. Each sturdy, straight stem with its dark-green leaves and white-spotted flowers will soon bear the heavy bean pods, but for a few sunny days, with the butterflies hovering over the blossoms, the field is an unforgettable sight.

You can well imagine that there is always something to watch and learn about in the farmer's fields. No two farms are alike, and each farmer must use his skill and experience to get the best crops from his land, and when you know a little more about farming you will know what to look for and what to admire.

* * *

WORKERS ON THE FARM

While you have been exploring the farm buildings and the fields you will have met some of the farmhands about their work, and I dare say you will have wondered how they manage to do all the jobs that have to be done, because they never seem to hurry.

For many years now in this country, we appear to have forgotten the man who works with his hands and whom we used to call a craftsman, and have paid more honour to scientists and engineers. Many foolish and ignorant people pretend to despise the slower-thinking countryman who has worked on the land all his life as did his father and grandfather before him. I want you to realise that you cannot enjoy the country unless you try to understand the men and women who live their lives and make their living in the country—simple people who are not interested in cinemas and streets and shops, but who, without ever saying much, are generally living very much happier lives than their brothers in the cities and towns, who never see the seasons change the fields and dress the trees each year anew.

You will find the men on the farm friendly enough if you don't get in their way, and so it is better for you to know what each does and how they set about their work. First, remember that they all work long hours and have very little leisure. It is true, of course, that they live near their work and do not, like the town dwellers, so often have a long journey to factory or office, but some farm workers are at work long before you are up, and at certain seasons, such as harvest, they are in the fields from dawn to moonrise.

Most farm workers have been trained to do several sorts of work with their hands, but as a rule the man in charge of the cows milks them and attends to them generally summer and winter and does not have time for much else.

If the farm is a big one, there will probably be a stockman, whose main job is to look after the horses and the heifers, but he would do many other jobs as well, according to the season of the year. Then there is sure to be one man in charge of the tractor, and he will probably be the ploughman as well. The powerful tractor has taken the place of the horse in many ways, and it is amazing to see how quickly a skilful man can plough a field with his tractor hauling a plough which turns four furrows at a time. But somehow the plough drawn by two strong horses is still a more impressive sight, and it is interesting to see how the ploughman here *follows* the plough, while the tractor driver must for ever be turning in his seat to see if his furrows are straight.

The shepherd is, of course, a real craftsman. *His* job cannot be learned out of a book, for his skill has come down to him from the days when our ancestors drove their flocks before them as they moved from camping-ground to settlement. It would need a complete book to tell you all that the shepherd does. He is a lonely, silent, kindly man who is not often seen about the farm itself. His hardest work is when the lambs are being born, between January and March, for then he never really leaves his sheep. He probably has a little hut on wheels which he moves near the lambing pen, and he attends every ewe when her lamb is born, because the very greatest care is taken by every good farmer of his sheep and lambs.

While the lambing pen is used it is the shepherd's work to find enough food for ewes, but of course, in wild country, such as Wales and Scotland, the lambs are born out on the hillsides and the shepherd has to do his best to find them and see that they come to no harm and do not fall into streams or down mountains.

Yes, the shepherd is a wonderful man, and if you can show him you are interested in his work, he will have lots to tell you. In the border hills of the North, he may have a flock of over six hundred sheep to care for, and he will certainly have, as a companion and helper, one of the famous sheep dogs. These dogs have an uncanny intelligence, and have been so well trained that they seem to understand their master's thoughts as they round up the wandering sheep and drive them into the fold.

* * *

HAYMAKING

In June the farmer cuts his hay, and this is one of the loveliest times of the year to be on a farm. The weather is generally hot and dry—for unless it is, he will not mow his fields—and the days are long, with glorious bright mornings and evenings when it seems a shame to be in bed. The lanes and hedgerows are thick with leaves and sweet-smelling blossoms, and in the hayfields the ripe grass waves gently in the summer breeze.

The farmer usually cuts the hay with a horse-drawn machine which is driven round the field with a cheerful sound as the hay falls in flat swathes to one side. The cut grass does not really become hay until it has been dried by the sun and the air, so there is still plenty to be done before it is ready to be stacked. First, the rows cut by the mowing machine are drawn into bigger rows either by hand or with a horse rake. After this the hay is turned and then the haycocks, or little round hillocks of hay, are made, and it is left like this for several days so that it may be thoroughly dry. When the farmer is satisfied that it is dry enough to cart, it is spread out again into the long rows—generally called windrows— and then along comes the waggon which the patient horse pulls slowly up the field and the workers toss the hay up to the man on the top.

You can help the farmer at haymaking-time by raking up the windrows and making haycocks and then spreading it out again before the waggon comes, and you can perhaps ride home on the top of it in state !

You may wonder why it is so important for the hay to be dry before it is carted and stacked. Have you ever noticed that when your lawn is cut at home and the grass cuttings are piled damp into a heap, they become very hot ? If the pile is big it may actually catch fire in the centre and smoulder, and the same would happen to a haystack which was damp when it was made. You can see how worrying it is for the farmer at haymaking-time, for he must judge the weather before he mows, hoping that the rain will keep off and the sun keep out to dry the windrows.

* * *

HARVEST

Long, long before the birth of Christ, when man worshipped strange gods, harvest was a time of festival and thanksgiving. It is, of course, to-day still the most important time in the farmer's calendar, for he now sees the result of all his anxious planning and work through the seasons. He has manured and ploughed in the autumn nearly a year ago, and he may have sown wheat within a few weeks of the ploughing and seen the sturdy, tender-looking shoots change the colour of his fields overnight. Then he has rolled the soil firm and seen the grain shoot up in the sunshine and rain of the spring. Sometimes, perhaps, the rain has come at the wrong time or there has been an early drought, and he has watched his fields anxiously. But the grain has grown, and generally in June the ear begins to show and the long green stalks stand like ranks of soldiers, which bend but do not break as the wind rustles over the fields.

And then, so gently that it seems as if a magic hand has touched them, the fields change colour and, where one day they were green, they now gleam like pale gold. As July deepens into August so does the standing grain ripen until the heads are heavy and drooping, and all the fields are glowing. Again the farmer must decide when to cut, and once he has made up his mind everybody on the farm, and indeed anyone who will help him, is called out into the fields from dawn until sunset, for as soon as the corn is cut the sheaves must be stooked—that is, stood upright with the ears of grain uppermost in groups of six, so that they may dry in the sun and the wind.

The machine which cuts the standing grain is called a binder, because it binds the sheaves with twine automatically as it circles the field. The binder is a heavy machine which is usually drawn by a tractor, and it can deal with a big field quickly. The cutting of the harvest is a thrilling experience, for as the binder whirrs round the golden field with its big wooden-bladed wheel beating down the grain on to the knives, the tied sheaves are flung out at the side. And while the golden rectangle in the middle of the field grows smaller the harvesters lift the sheaves and pile them into stooks, until they stand like little houses on the stubble. When a strip only a few yards wide remains to be cut the farmer and his friends fetch their guns and stand at the corners to wait for the panic-stricken rabbits who now dash madly for the shelter of the hedgerows. Bang! Bang! go the guns and down go the rabbits, and although I shall have something to tell you about

27

these harmless-looking little animals later on, you should understand now that you needn't be sorry for rabbits and think it cruel to shoot them. Rabbits on a farm are a pest and a danger and responsible for much damage.

The stooks must stand in the fields until the farmer is certain that the grain is dry enough to be carried. Sometimes, if there is not much sun, they may have to wait for three weeks before the waggons come and the sheaves are carried to the stackyard. You can see that it is much easier to cart tied sheaves than loose hay, and if there are plenty of workers the fields can soon be cleared.

And so you see harvest-time is the end of the farmer's year, and it must be wonderful for him to see the last load sway out through the gate in the hedge and to know that all his work and planning have been worth while and that it is a " good harvest." In olden times—and indeed on many farms now— " Harvest Home," as it was called, was a time of great rejoicing. Friends and neighbours sat down to a gigantic supper with the farm workers and their wives, and in this way the farmer would say " Thank you " to those who had helped him. A week or two later, perhaps, the farmer and his family may be seen going to the village church, which will be suitably decorated with sheaves of corn and Michaelmas daisies and marrows, to give thanks to God for His blessings on Harvest Festival Day.

*　　　*　　　*

If after reading a little about what goes on at a farm you feel you would like to know more about farming or be a farmer yourself one day, there are plenty of books to read, and some of them are listed in the special section later in this book. You may also like to know that there is an organisation called the National Federation of Young Farmers Clubs and that boys and girls between the ages of ten and twenty-one can become members if they are interested. You can write to the Secretary, N.F.Y.F.C., Selwyn House, Endsleigh Street, London, W.C.1, for full particulars.

*　　　*　　　*

And so " Farewell to the Farm," in the words written by Robert Louis Stevenson, who also wrote *Treasure Island* and *Kidnapped* and lots of other splendid books which you must be sure to read for yourself. When he wrote these verses there were obviously no cars, but I expect the farm he was thinking about then looks much the same to-day and will not look very different in twenty years' time.

FAREWELL TO THE FARM

The coach is at the door at last ;
The eager children, mounting fast
And kissing hands, in chorus sing :
Good-bye, good-bye, to everything !

The house and garden, field and lawn,
The meadow-gates we swang upon,
To pump and stable, tree and swing,
Good-bye, good-bye, to everything !

And fare you well for evermore,
O ladder at the hayloft door,
O hayloft where the cobwebs cling,
Good-bye, good-bye, to everything !

Crack goes the whip, and off we go ;
The trees and houses smaller grow ;
Last, round the woody turn we swing :
Good-bye, good-bye, to everything !

ROBERT LOUIS STEVENSON

The Village

THE CITY CHILD

Dainty little maiden, whither would you wander ?
Whither from this pretty home, the home where mother dwells ?
" Far and far away," said the dainty little maiden,
" All among the gardens, auriculas, anemones,
Roses and lilies and Canterbury-bells."

Dainty little maiden, whither would you wander ?
Whither from this pretty house, this city house of ours ?
" Far and far away," said the dainty little maiden,
" All among the meadows, the clover and the clematis,
Daisies and kingcups and honeysuckle-flowers."

ALFRED TENNYSON

THESE verses were written in the last century by a great
English poet at a time when our towns and cities were even
dirtier and dingier than they are to-day, but I dare say that
if you live in a town you have often felt you too would like
to wander far away and find the " daisies and kingcups and
honeysuckle-flowers."

It is said that eight out of every ten of our people live
in the towns and cities, and because of this it is important
for you to realise that although most townspeople are very
proud of their shops and cinemas and streets and parks,
the ordinary town is really something new in England.
Our big industrial towns grew as workmen left the villages in
which they were born to earn more money in the new factories
which sprang up without any planning as machinery became
available.

We explored the farm together first because we generally
think of the farm as the country, and indeed sometimes we
should find that the farm might well have been the beginning

of the village. But it is in the villages of our land that you will find our real history. When you get to know country people better you will understand a little why it is that they seem so tranquil and unhurried and why time does not seem so important as it does to the town dweller, who has a bus or a train to catch and is always looking at his watch. Many of our villages belong to the early history of our country and were there when the Romans arrived. Even if you are not a very learned person, but were born and brought up and work in such a village, you cannot help feeling that you really " belong " there. And the important thing to remember about an English village is that however small it may be it is, even now, nearly self-contained and that most of its inhabitants only leave it once a week to go shopping on market day. They do not really mind whether visitors go or stay, for unless your family has lived there for hundreds of years they will look upon you as " strangers " because you do not " belong."

I don't suppose there are two villages actually alike in all our land, but there are certain characteristics common to every village, so let us pretend that you are going to spend a holiday in a village to which you have never been before, and I will try to tell you what to look for and how to do some real exploring. If you come by train, the railway station will probably be at the nearest market town. From here you will perhaps take the country bus, and it will be crowded if it happens to be market day—but try to wedge yourself in a corner next to the window and look round and listen till it is time to start. As the bus fills up with these jolly country people, who are quite unlike the rather worried-looking folk you see on the trams at home, you realise that they all know each other and each other's families and business.

The women clamber up the bus steps with their baskets of shopping and all have a smile and a word for the driver who is enjoying a cigarette outside. There are not many men about because they have market business to be conducted over a friendly pint of beer, but there are a few children who have come from the Grammar School, and they are certainly wondering what you are doing in their bus. At last you start off down the narrow street, made narrower by the square market building planted right in the middle. Then the bus lurches up and over a narrow bridge and turns left at a cross-roads and you have left the little town behind and are in the country and running along between hedges. The road is little more than a lane and is awkward for driving, because it has many dangerous corners and seems to wander all over the countryside like a crazy, fairy road. But this road was a track hundreds of years ago, and if you watch carefully you will see how it links up lonely farms and hamlets with the villages. The bus is emptying now, for it stops at nearly every cross-roads and farm. Sometimes the conductor leaves a parcel at a shop or an inn and both he and the driver have a cheerful " Goodnight " for every departing passenger and a greeting for everyone on the road whom they know.

Now the conductor warns you that you're nearly at your journey's end. The road is running downhill through an avenue of beech trees and below you the setting sun is gilding the weathercock on the top of a square, grey church tower which stands high above a cluster of red roofs. The bus slows down as a herd of brown and white Jersey cows crosses the road from pasture into a farm gate. A small boy is urging the cows with a stick as big as himself, and he winks at the driver as he whacks the last cow over the road. Then the road crosses a stream and you see a stretch of common surrounded by elm trees, above which a black cloud of rooks is wheeling. Then some cottages with walled gardens ablaze with colour, then the school house, then a cross-roads, then a sharp turn to the left and you are in a cobbled square with the great church dominating all and your friends waiting to welcome you at the bus stop, outside the shop which is also a post office. You have arrived.

*   *   *

THE CHURCH

The history of the village will be found in its church, which will almost certainly be the oldest building in the village, and

I am one of the people who is quite certain that it was and is still the most important.

Now the building of our old churches and cathedrals was a very wonderful and exciting business, because the men who built them actually worked for the glory of God, and because it was *their* church that they were building they rarely did any slipshod or careless work, but gave of their very best. Rich and poor alike shared in the work, and I suppose that the former gave the money while the latter worked with their hands, but of course they had to call in skilled carvers and stonemasons as well, and these craftsmen must have been a happy lot of men, for they spent their lives working to beautify the houses of God.

You will notice that the church is generally built on the highest ground in the village, and there are several reasons for this. The first and most logical reason is that the church was in those days not only the centre of community life, but was rightly recognised as God's house which must stand above all else in the village. The other reason is more practical. The tower of the church was an admirable lookout spot, which was so necessary in the wild days when our distant ancestors were struggling to establish their homes and their church. But however the church was built, it is important to remember that these splendid ancestors of ours put God and His worship above all else and were never satisfied until their churches were built as strongly and beautifully as possible.

Not every church is beautiful, for many have been spoiled by clumsy repairs and some were robbed and deliberately made ugly by Cromwell's soldiers, but every one is interesting. Don't be shy about going into a church and looking round. If you do not know someone who will act as your guide, see if you can find the rector and ask him. He'll probably be glad to find someone who is interested, and when he has shown you the church he may take you up the tower and let you see the great bells which in olden times used to ring out warnings, besides calling people to worship. To reach the church you must go through the churchyard, which is sometimes called " God's Acre." It may have a lych-gate—a wooden gate under a sloping wooden roof—and it may boast one or two yew trees planted at the time the church was first built many hundreds of years ago. On the tombstones in the churchyard you can read, if you will, the names of those who lived and died in this place through the centuries. Again and again you will read the same names—names that probably you will see painted over the few shop fronts, over the inn doors and on the sides of farm carts in the street outside.

Before you go into the church, look at the great thickness of the walls and remember that when it was built it might sometimes have to be used as a fortress. But although the outside may look old you will probably find the interior much older. Many churches have a table just inside the door on which there may be a book or a leaflet giving the history of the church and the interesting things to look for, but if there is nothing to help you will have to look round for yourself.

There is no room here to tell you how to recognise by the stonework and types of windows and arches and the like when the church was built, but there is a very good book about this which I recommend to you in the Book Section presently. But you should look first at the stained-glass windows. If any of these are old, look carefully in the corner and you may see that the artist has painted in some local scene or custom as a background to his main subject. Look at the walls and see whether there are any traces of painting here, and remember that hundreds of years ago, when nobody could read or write, it was often by pictures that the Church taught her people the story of the Gospel. Then look for other work of old craftsmen at the font, where the stonework may be beautifully carved, and you can spare a moment to remember that here, on this spot, mothers and fathers of the village have brought their children to be baptised and made members of God's family. At the ends of the choir stalls, and sometimes at the backs of the seats themselves, you may find all sorts of carvings. If you are lucky, you may find the jolliest figures carved here—knights and ladies, crusaders, jesters, and sometimes such a collection of ugly, grotesque faces, that you can almost imagine a jolly little

34

wood carver in the fourteenth century sitting down where you are standing now and saying to himself, " I can't think of any more Saints, but I've got three more heads to do, so for a start I'll do that old woman who shouted at me so rudely down by the brook."

Then there will be brass plates and monuments to look at, and there may be some old pictures too. Look under the tower for the bellropes, but don't touch them, and look, too, for bricked-up windows and doors and places where the original building has been altered.

Nowhere else in the village will you find so much history in so small a space. Where you now stand, generation after generation of British yeomen and their families have come in from the fields and houses outside to thank God for His mercies.

So you will see why it is a good idea to start exploring the village at the church.

*   *   *

SQUIRE AND PARSON

After the church the two most imposing buildings in the village are likely to be the Rectory and the big house which is generally known as the Manor House.

Both will have been built at a time when rector and squire were the actual leaders of the village, for the priest looked after his people's spiritual welfare and the squire owned all the land—he would probably be a descendant of the old barons—and employed nearly all the people and owned their houses as well. As you know, it is rather different now. Both houses will probably be interesting, with big gardens and orchards and very often with stables too. The Rectory is, of course, near the church, but the Manor may be some distance away. If the Manor is very old, there may be traces of fortifications, because, in a village, the Manor House was often built to withstand attack from outlaws and robbers. But most of the Manor Houses of England are memorials of a quiet and gracious way of living in beautiful surroundings.

There may be some lovely things to see in these two houses, and perhaps there are ghosts haunting the echoing corridors of the Manor and a secret passage in the Rectory.

* * *

INNS

In the village there are two recognised meeting-places for all the people—the church and the inn. Sometimes the inn may be as old as the church, but like the church it is not now used in quite the same way. There are times of the day now when the doors of the inn are barred, but even if you are not allowed to cross the threshold, you can look at the swinging sign and see by the walls and the type of building whether the inn is as old as the Manor House. The landlord—he used to be called " Mine Host " but now he's more likely to be called " The Guvnor "—will know everybody, and on Saturday evenings in particular, when his house is packed with farm workers from miles around, the inn will be a very jolly place with the air blue with smoke and loud with gossip and laughter.

If you are ever lucky enough to stay in an old inn, you may find it difficult not to lose your way in its winding passages and creaking stairs. At the side there is often a gateway leading to a cobbled yard and stables where the farmers used to put up their horses. Of course, the biggest inns are to be found in the market towns, but your village will have at least one, and if it is clean and well kept it will play a very big part in the life of the people.

* * *

THE VILLAGE SHOP

There's nothing quite like the English village shop any-where else in the world. If you've come to stay in the village, you cannot miss the shop, because it sells everything that you can possibly want, including stamps and postal orders. I remember that as a very little boy I used to be rather scared of the dark low-ceilinged cave to which I was sometimes sent for sweets, clutching two hot pennies in my hand. A bell jangled madly when the door was opened, and at once I felt awkward and shy because I couldn't see anybody, and yet things were all round me, so that I fell over them, and hanging from the ceiling, so that I had to duck, were cards of men's braces and some strings of Spanish onions. There was an old, old woman whom I believed to be a witch who sometimes came to serve me, and I remember that her pale face used to appear like magic in a blank space above the counter. And I expect it's just the same to-day ! Packed to the doors with flour and tins of biscuits and men's shirts and rabbit snares and jars of sweets and a picture-postcard stand and black farming boots and cigarettes and a thousand and one things, before you can even find the little cage where the old witch sits on her broomstick and sells stamps.

Perhaps there won't be a witch in your village shop, but I should look carefully !

*　　　*　　　*

THE PEOPLE OF THE VILLAGE

If you live in a town or suburb, you will probably wonder what all the people who live in a village really do. There may be only three hundred people in the parish, but if you are used to seeing your father and perhaps elder brothers and sisters rush off to catch trains or trams every morning to go to work, it is rather hard to realise that the villager lives a full and useful life without moving very far from his cottage door. There are no factories in the village, although, of course, in some parts of the country there might be quarries or brick fields nearby where a number are employed, but generally the village is the centre of a number of farms, and it is on the farms that most of the men are employed.

We have already mentioned that the Parson and Squire are still, in a way, the leaders of the village, but although most of the farmers will live outside the village, they are very important members of the community, and everyone will respect them because their names are probably the oldest in the village and they are doing what their fathers did.

Then there is the Schoolmaster and his family. Perhaps his wife teaches in the school as well, and you can be sure that they are both important people, because all the children in the village come under their influence, and if they do their work well parents will respect them too and ask their help in many ways. The schoolmaster is sure to be invited to take part in all the village activities, and he is probably the most overworked man in the place.

Besides the schoolmaster there are two more men who are paid for their work from the money which comes from taxes— the Policeman and the Postman. The postman is everybody's friend, for he knows every house and cottage and farm for miles around and knows all about everybody's joys and sorrows. Through scorching, dusty summers and bitter winters he makes his daily round, pushing his old bicycle over field paths where he cannot ride. To many he is the only link with the outside world, and sometimes he will help by bringing the daily paper or messages from friends at some distant farm. The country postman often knows more about the lives of those he visits than does the parson.

The policeman knows everybody, too, but he does not visit so many homes. He probably has many miles to travel each week and perhaps another village to look after. He will be known well on all the farms, but country folk are very honest and great respecters of other's property, and it is not likely that he will have much to do besides keeping a lookout for poachers.

Another helpful person whom you will see cycling about the lanes is the district nurse, and she too probably knows the inside of every house and cottage for miles around. In the country the doctor has many villages to look after and often lives too far away for his patients to call, so it is the district nurse who is sent for first in most cases of illness. Everybody knows her and trusts her, and she has probably seen every child in the village born.

Then there are the tradesmen who make a living by supplying the farmers and their workers with bread and meat and groceries. Almost every village now has its own garage, and the man who runs this will be a very busy person, for not only will he repair cars and sell petrol and oil, but he may drive a car of his own for hire and mend the bicycles of the village when he has the time. Although the big shops in the market towns do attract many of the villagers now that the bus makes it easier for them to do an afternoon's shopping, the village tradesman has an important part to play and manages to hold his own in spite of deliveries by motor vans from the towns. People still like dealing with people they have known all their lives, and this is particularly true in the village.

*　　*　　*

THE CRAFTSMEN

There are not many craftsmen left in the villages now, but in some parts of the country you will still find a special craft being practised as it has been done for hundreds of years in the same place. The women lace-makers of Honiton are an example of this, as are the weavers of the Hebrides who make the world-famous Harris tweed.

But almost every village has its carpenter, who can make a good living, and there may still be a blacksmith in his forge. In the days when every farmer was dependent upon his horses both for working his fields and for transport for himself and his family, the smith was a very important man and his craft is likely to be the oldest in the place. Perhaps he does not have to work so hard now as his father did, but there is still plenty for him to do besides his main work of shoeing horses, for he is a useful man to mend a piece of machinery, or to make hinges for country gates. All the farm carts have iron " tyres " or hoops on their wheels, and although these take a long time to wear out, only the blacksmith can put them on in the first place, because it requires great skill and practice to do this properly.

The forge is a dark, dirty and exciting place, and you should certainly make friends with the smith and go and see him at his work. The fire which heats the iron is raised off the floor to a convenient height and is a heap of small coal and coke which is fanned into white heat by a big bellows. The iron bar on the fire soon glows too, and when it is soft enough the smith whips it out with long pincers, holds it over the pointed end of the anvil and hammers it into shape. Much work goes into the making of one shoe, but the smith is so quick and strong that you will have to watch carefully to see how he shapes the ridge for the square-headed nails. The bellows cough, the fire roars and the sparks fly as the great hammer comes down accurately on the glowing iron with a merry clanging which is music to the true countryman.

Horses never seem to mind being shod, and of course they cannot feel either the hot shoe when it is first tried on or the nails that hold it in place. Notice how the smith takes the horse's hoof between his own legs, which hold it firm while he fits on the hot shoe which trims and marks the hoof so that he can see whether it is too big or too small. Once more he heats and hammers and then flings the shoe into cold water to cool before it is finally nailed on.

The forge is a jolly place to spend an hour, and the smith a good friend to make because he knows everybody, as his father did before him. The horses know him, too, and he knows all of them and their habits as well. Although the forge may seem to you to be in a fearful muddle, the smith knows where everything is and why it is there. If you watched him carefully, you would see that the handle of the bellows was close to his left hand and the water was below the fire, where it is easy for him to drop in the horseshoe without moving about. Generations of smiths before him found out the best and easiest way of working, and he still works in the same way.

*   *   *

In some parts of the country they have been making bricks for hundreds of years, and so there will be many brick-makers in the village who make these bricks better than anyone from another part of the country would do. Some villages are skilled in basket-making, others in quarrying and others in indoor crafts, but you will soon notice that the particular craft of your village depends upon the country in which it is set.

How Walking-sticks are Made

Haven't you often wondered whether walking-sticks grow with straight or rounded handles, or whether they are made that way ? There is a village in Surrey where there is a walking-stick " factory " and where many thousands of ash sticks are growing, and this is how it is done. First the " seeds " of the ash tree which fall in the summer and autumn—the country children call them " keys," and I expect you have seen them as they come fluttering down—are sown in long rows. When each seedling is big enough it is taken up and replanted *lengthways* in the ground, so that it now grows in two different directions—one underground on the root and the other straight up at right angles to the root. The second growth comes from a bud in the tiny sapling under the ground struggling to grow upwards to the sun and air. These little sticks are now left to grow like this for three or four years. When they are finally dug up, the root, cut short, becomes the handle and the big new growth that sprang from the buried bud is the stick. There is still plenty to be done, of course, before the sticks are sent to the shops, and skilled craftsmen cut off the knots and polish the bare patches, shape the handle a little if necessary, and thin down the end of the stick and fix the ferrule.

So you see it takes at least five years to make an ash walking-stick, but this " factory " is a very good example of village industry or craftsmanship.

* * *

The Village Green

Every village should have a village green, and most have a piece of precious common land which, for hundreds of years, has belonged to the people and where they are free to come and go as they please, and use to graze their goats or their geese. Once a maypole was set up once a year on the sward, but now there is hardly a village green in the land where cricket is not played, as it has been played for as long as the game has existed. Cricket was born on a village green in Hampshire, and there are many countrymen who still maintain that it is only on the rough pitches of these greens that cricket is played as it should be played. Foreigners are bewildered by the Englishman's enthusiasm for the game, but village cricket is part of our way of living, and a Saturday afternoon match between two neighbouring villages is a very exciting and serious affair. Butcher, baker, squire and parson, blacksmith and garage man and the gardener from the Manor may all be in the team. The old men of the village sit on benches under the trees and mumble to each other about the good old days when cricket *was* cricket. The cheerful clatter of tea-cups comes from the pavilion and an excited small boy changes the figures on the score board as the wickets fall. And after tea, when the visiting team are the guests, and the shadows from the elms are lengthening and the rooks set up their evening clamour and the little crowd round the ring has grown—then, as the batsmen fight for runs and the fielders close in and the hands of the clock creep on—then, if you are old enough and sensible enough to understand, you will realise that cricket is part of England's heritage and that it belongs to the village.

* * *

FLOWER SHOWS

Another jolly feature of village life is the Flower Show, and you should certainly go to one if you can. Most village flower shows used to be held on August Bank Holiday, and some-times they are in aid of the nearest hospital. Almost every-one in the village will enter something and the trestle tables in the marquees will be groaning under the entries of giant vegetable marrows, potatoes, cauliflowers, runner beans and onions. There will probably be classes for honey and eggs, and maybe a prize offered for the best bunch of wild flowers. The judges have a very difficult task, for it takes a brave man to decide that for the first time for six years the parson is not going to win the first prize for onions and that he has been beaten by the sexton, who has been waiting and working for this very moment for nine years !

Sometimes there are sports for the children, too, and perhaps pony rides, and later on, after the prizes have been presented by Mrs. Squire, there may be dancing for the grown-ups.

* * *

You have probably learned by now that the jolliest things in life are nearly always the things you do with other people, and for a long time it has been obvious that man has nearly lost the gift of living in neighbourliness with his neighbours. You may know that it is possible to live for many years in a town street without knowing the people next door, and indeed many families do live in such unnatural loneliness.

But such a state is impossible in a village which is hundreds of years old. Everybody knows everybody else, and that, I think, is why country life is such a reality. It is so much easier for people who live and work and play together in a small place to share their interests, and that is why a flower show in the Vicarage garden is often a jollier and friendlier affair than a bazaar in a Church Hall, and why a cricket match on the village green seems more like a real game than the staid, professionally staged matches in a park.

But we shall have to guard our villages very carefully, and that is why I have tried to explain what the village means in the life of us all, even if we have to live in a town. One day you will be old enough to decide who is going to represent you in Parliament. That is a big responsibility ; somebody has got to see, for the sake of the community, that good farming land is not sold to builders, that houses are not built without considering their surroundings, that common land is not stolen from the people, and that rural factories are not ugly.

It is important, too, to remember that every village must provide for its own worship, education and amusement.

* * *

We started this section with a poem called " The City Child," written in the last century. Now we come to some more lovely verses written by a modern poet who chose the same title. Have you ever felt that you wanted to walk and walk far beyond where the trams stop above the grimy town ? If you walk far enough, or if you go in your caravan with its blue wheels, you'll reach the village at last.

THE CITY CHILD

When I grow up, I will not live
  In a dull house in a dull row,
Where feathers of smoke from tall chimneys
  Are the only beautiful things I know.

No, indeed ! I'll follow uphill
  The trams that lead to a far moor-top ;
When I get there, I'll rest awhile,
  Then walk for hours without a stop,

Till I find a beck with no tin cans,
  Where flowers are clean and trees are high ;
It's there I will have a big caravan
  With wheels as blue as a picture sky.

I'll have a horse—the old brown horse
  Who is tired of pulling the brewer's dray
Up the cobbled street in the choky fog,—
  And I'll give him apples four times a day.

At dusk no mill shall block out the stars,
  And I will not sleep ; but all night thro'
On my caravan steps I'll sit and think
  Of the wonderful things there are to do.

DOROTHY UNA RATCLIFFE

Animals of the Countryside

WHEN you go for a walk in the town you are not likely to see any animals except dogs and cats, and perhaps a rather sad-looking horse pulling a milk-cart. In the country, every walk will be an adventure when you realise that the fields, hedgerows and woods are rustling with wild life, and when you have learned how to keep still and watch the movement going on around you. It would take many books much bigger than this to describe all the animals still to be found in our country, and as this is only a scrap-book I can only tell you a little here about the animals you might see on any country walk. Remember that many people grow up without ever having learned how to see what is going on around them, and that wild animals have grown very shy and fearful of men. If you would like to learn to read Nature, you must be patient and gentle, and remember that animals, like humans, are all different, and not nearly so lazy !

* * *

RABBITS

The harmless-looking rabbit is likely to be the animal you will see most often on a country walk, particularly if you are abroad in the evening. Rabbits live in colonies in underground burrows called warrens, and on a warm evening in the summer they come out and sit in the sunshine while the baby rabbits play around them. If you make a noise, you will see one or two of the older and wiser ones thump on the grass with their strong back legs. This is a danger signal, and in a flash and with a scurry of white bob-tails the entire colony will disappear underground again.

The rabbit is a pest. He belongs to the same family as the rat—the rodent or gnawing family—and although he is not quite the nuisance to the farmer that he used to be, he should be looked upon as vermin, for he does terrible damage to the food crops, and indeed all that he seems to leave behind him is weeds, although he will eat some of these when he is hungry. He will gnaw through saplings in the woods, steal the lettuces and cabbages in gardens if he can get in, and spoil a field with his burrowing under and through the hedges. He does not like the wet and stays underground when it rains. The best times to watch rabbits are in the early morning or at dusk, when they come out to feed. The mother rabbit—she is called a doe—has several large families a year, and she is a good and affectionate mother. Nevertheless, the farmer will shoot her when he can, for she is good to eat, and a menace to him. It seems rather a pity that the rabbit is such an attractive little animal to watch as he lollops through the woods or plays in the sunshine, but although he is timid, with very acute hearing, he is not difficult to find, for he breeds anywhere—in woods, on the mountain-side and in the hedgerows and fields.

* * *

RATS

Sometimes, as you walk softly down the lane you will hear a rustle in the ditch, and if you are quick enough you may see a long-tailed brown rat squirming through the hedge. There are millions of rats in this country, and they are a far greater menace to man than the rabbit, for besides destroying crops, damaging stored food, stealing eggs, gnawing holes in barns and nesting in the ricks, they carry disease. There is no greater enemy among our wild animals than the rat, and he must be exterminated. You can often hear rats scuttling and squealing round a stack in the evening, but they also live in burrows and manure heaps. They are extremely cunning and very brave fighters, and sometimes have been known to turn and face a terrier. The mother rat often has over one hundred babies a year, so you can see how important it is to kill them all. There are some odd stories told about rats, and I expect you have heard the phrase about " rats deserting the sinking ship." Sailors declare that when rats leave a ship it is doomed, and it is true that sometimes rats will decide without apparent reason to leave the place in which they have made their homes, and hundreds of them will cross roads and fields to found a new colony elsewhere. Perhaps Robert Browning knew this when he wrote the story-poem, which I expect you know, called " The Pied Piper of Hamelin."

> . . . And out of the houses the rats came tumbling,
> Great rats, small rats, lean rats, brawny rats,
> Brown rats, black rats, grey rats, tawny rats,
> Grave old plodders, gay young friskers,
>   Fathers, mothers, uncles, cousins,
> Cocking tails and pricking whiskers,
>   Families by tens and dozens,
> Brothers, sisters, husbands, wives—
> Followed the Piper for their lives. . . .

*   *   *

SQUIRRELS

The squirrel is another member of the rodent family, and you will see him in the woods where he lives and makes his home in the tree tops. There are two kinds in the British Isles now—the red and the grey. The first is a timid but attractive little chap, but the grey squirrel is becoming a nuisance, for he is increasing rapidly, and because he is bigger and stronger than his little red cousin, the latter may soon become extinct. The grey squirrel is a greedy thief, and will break birds' eggs in the nests and even eat fledglings. He nibbles at the bark of trees and destroys buds and young shoots. Many farmers shoot him at sight.

The little red squirrel is not nearly so destructive, and lives almost entirely on nuts and seeds. When you walk through the woods, look at the foot of trees for empty nut shells and pine cones, which is a sign that a squirrel has been enjoying a meal. Then look up and, high in the branches, you may see the squirrel's home, which is called a

" drey," and is made like a magpie's nest. Seen from below it looks like an untidy collection of dead leaves and old sticks, but it is a real house, and serves as a bedroom and a nursery, and sometimes as a castle which has to be vigorously defended.

It is commonly believed that squirrels go to sleep all the winter like dormice—this is called hibernating—but this is not true. On the coldest winter day in the woods you can sometimes see a squirrel hunting for food, and he is certainly very amusing to watch as he holds a nut or an acorn in his front paws and sits up to eat it. In the autumn, squirrels work harder than ever, and although they eat twice as much as usual and grow very fat, they also find time to bury some of their food, and what is particularly odd is that sometimes they bury their nuts and acorns singly and in different places all over the wood. It is obviously impossible for them to remember where the stores are hidden, but at least this method of distributing seeds does help to keep the forests growing, for new oaks and hazels will spring up where the squirrel has planted seeds.

Squirrels are noisy little animals, and you will often hear them before you see them. They have a queer call which starts with a screech and ends with something like a mew; sometimes they just chatter. They are always intensely busy, darting up and down the tree trunks or swinging, almost like monkeys, across the wood in the tree tops.

* * *

THE HARE

The hare is also a rodent, of course, and a sort of big brother to the rabbit, although he does not do as much damage. He is a big fellow, with powerful hind legs, and big ears which stand upright when he is on the alert for danger, and lie flat against his head when he is racing over the fields. You will remember that he is a very fast runner, although he leaps rather more than runs. Unlike the rabbit, he does not live underground, and the mother hare does not even bother to make a special nest for her babies, but merely

The grain is cut, the sheaves are ready to be stooked, the binder goes home.

The Inn is one of the chief meeting-places of village and market town. The busy market-day scene on the left shows Mr. and Mrs. Farmer buying, selling and chatting. Country people have always made more time for meeting than the townsman, and the lives of English yeomen—men like the old ploughman below and his ancestors for centuries before him—have centred round these places.

This village may have started before the Normans came to England! No two villages are alike, although each has grown up in its own way around the Church or Manor House until it seems to be part of the countryside.

We call the Oak the "King of the Trees"— most of the ancient forests that covered our land were of oak and the wood used to build the British Navy.

chooses a hollow—technically called a " form "—in long grass or in the middle of a ploughed field. The male hare also uses a form in which he will sit all day with his red-brown fur blending with the background, and making him practically invisible. In the evening he will move off to find his supper of grasses and roots and vegetables—if he can steal them—from a nearby garden, and come back to his " form " in the morning. The mother hare, like the rabbit, is called a doe, the father a buck, or Jack hare, and the babies are known as leverets.

In the spring, which is the mating time, the bucks perform the most amazing antics, and will rise up on their back legs and box with their forefeet any other buck which dares to come near the doe. Sometimes in March they dash madly about the fields seeking a fight, and I think it must have been these antics which led to the saying, " mad as a March hare."

Not until you have seen a hare in full flight is it possible for you to realise how fast an animal can run. Except for the mating time, the hare lives alone, and is always seen alone. He is also an excellent and courageous swimmer.

*　　*　　*

The Fox

There is no more fascinating animal in our countryside than the fox. He is handsome, intelligent, courageous, cunning, arrogant and greedy. He is a menace to the farmer, for he will kill and steal chickens, geese, and even young lambs, and yet he is held in great respect by all those who hunt him for pleasure. He lives in the woods and makes his " earth " in a rabbit's burrow. His coat is a rich " autumn red," but he moves so silently and quickly that he is difficult to see. Sometimes if you listen carefully in the country in winter, you can hear him bark—rather a high-pitched bark, but unmistakable—as he covers many miles of country to find a mate. The baby foxes are generally born in May and June, and are as attractive as puppies. The mother-fox—called a vixen—feels her responsibilities keenly, but both father and mother take a share in training the cubs to fend for themselves. If you are ever lucky enough to see a family of foxes at play in the sunshine of a summer evening, you will realise how domesticated they are.

Foxes are flesh-eaters, and will eat meat dead or alive. They are particularly fond of poultry, and every wise country-man locks up his chickens at night, as Reynard is cunning enough to come back night after night for his favourite meal.

He is a very clever hunter, and it is said that he can actually mimic other animals' voices. Sometimes you will see him fascinating rabbits by gambolling and playing in front of them until he gets near enough to pounce. The rabbit, being both inquisitive and silly, always stays to watch this curious exhibition, and then, of course, is trapped. It is true that the fox will hunt and eat rats if he has to do so, but he doesn't seem to like them as much as rabbits.

Many people disagree about the hunting of the fox with riders and packs of hounds. There was not much hunting in wartime, and many farmers had to shoot the foxes on their land, but whether hunting is cruel or not, the fox is an enemy of man, and does no good beyond the killing of rabbits and sometimes a few rats.

He really is worth looking for, though, and the best time is the evening, when he comes out to hunt for himself and his family. You may see him trotting like a dusky shadow down the side of the wood, or in the ditch below the hedge. He moves fast and silently—ears cocked and white-tipped tail held low.

* * *

STOATS AND WEASELS

A few years ago, stoats and weasels were usually classed as vermin, and the gamekeeper would kill all he could find and hang up the bodies as a " warning " to all other wild animals and birds who might destroy the eggs or kill the fledglings, which, later in the year, were to be killed by sportsmen's guns! But now, when pheasants and part-ridges are not so important, farmers are beginning to realise that both these blood-thirsty little hunters are friends rather than enemies because they kill *real* vermin—rats, mice and rabbits. Stoats and weasels are the rat's greatest enemies.

The stoat is a little red-brown animal about twelve inches long, with a blunt head and short ears. He has a long, black-tipped, and not very bushy tail, and short legs. No animal for its size is braver than the stoat. He is a real hunter, who does not wait for dusk, and may often be seen in the middle of a lane or field-path in broad daylight. The stoat nests in tree stumps, banks, molehills, or old walls. He is intensely inquisitive, and even if you surprise him, and he takes cover for a minute, he will soon pop up his head again, and peer at you with little bright eyes. Having marked down his prey he will follow it tirelessly through water, up and down a tree, or even into an unknown burrow, without the slightest trace of fear. He never seems to tire, and he swims as well as he runs. Another interesting thing about the stoat is that he has learned to hunt in packs, and sometimes you can see the astonishing sight of twelve or more of these little animals out hunting together. A pack of stoats has been known to attack a dog, and even a man, when either attempted to drive them from their prey.

It is an extraordinary thing that stoats, and weasels too, have an unexplainable power over animals many times their weight, and many times faster. Both hares and rabbits, in particular, are sometimes paralysed with fear, and crouch waiting for their dreaded enemy to pounce.

In the colder parts of the British Isles—and particularly in Scotland—the stoat changes the colour of his coat to pure white, except for the black tip to his tail, in the winter months. He is then called the ermine and, of course, is practically invisible against the snow.

The weasel is much like his cousin, the stoat, but he is a little smaller, his tail is shorter and his muzzle is perhaps more pointed. He is just as bloodthirsty, and kills more than he can eat, and will sometimes be seen dragging home a carcass much bigger than himself.

"BROCK" THE BADGER

Perhaps the most delightful animal of our countryside is the badger. He belongs to the same family as the stoat, but he is not often seen now, and only seldom in daylight. He is quite a big animal, and is nearly three feet in length, grey, with a white head striped with black. He has strong, sharp forepaws, with which he digs himself an amazing home underground, called a holt. This holt has numerous "rooms" on different levels, with several entrances and exits, and is sometimes shared with a family of foxes. He lives in the woods and on the wild hillsides, and although gentle, will fight fiercely if attacked. Badgers are wonderful parents, and they make the most delightful and amusing pets, and, with patience, are fairly easily tamed. Like the hedgehog, they sleep all the winter, and no other animal has cleaner habits. Although they eat rabbits, young birds and moles, they also enjoy roots and fruits and honey and insects.

Just because "Brock" is rather rare now, it is worth taking a lot of trouble to see him.

*　　　*　　　*

THE HEDGEHOG

The hedgehog is the oddest-looking animal to be found in our countryside. Instead of fur he has a coat of short, prickly spines, so sharp that you will cut yourself if you try to pick him up or uncurl him when he has rolled himself into a ball. This is what he does to protect himself, for he is a timid and inoffensive little animal who modestly keeps under hedges and eats all sorts of garden pests. As he wanders along in the dusk his spines lie flat against his back, but at the slightest sign of danger he rolls himself up tight, with his nose and legs and tail hidden, and with the spines forming a coat of armour. Strangely enough, the spines also act as a sort of cushion, for he can roll down a hill or drop from a very considerable height without hurt. He sleeps all day and all the winter, too—sometimes from November until May. Like the squirrel, he eats tremendously in the autumn, and makes himself extra fat. Country people welcome " fuzzypeg " in their gardens because he eats slugs, snails, beetles, insects and frogs. He is also particularly fond of snakes, and will attack an adder without fear, grabbing it by the tail and then rolling himself into a ball while the snake tears itself to pieces by striking at his spines.

Sometimes in the daytime you can hear him snoring under a hedge, but he doesn't wake up and trot along the ditches until it is nearly dark.

* * *

THE MOLE

Everybody has seen the piles of soil thrown up over fields and sometimes in gardens by the mole. You will not often see this little old gentleman in his velvet coat, because he lives almost entirely underground. He is about six inches long, with a square, strong snout and very strong forepaws, with strangely human-looking " hands " set sideways. Sometimes he pops his head out of a molehill to take a look round, but he is very timid, and will burrow down into the soft earth immediately when he hears or smells you. He is too blind to see more than a few inches, and this is not surprising, as he lives in darkness. His life is one long, desperate search for food, for he starves to death in only a few hours if he cannot find the worms and grubs he needs, and that is why he is always burrowing just underneath the surface. All the little underground passages he makes lead back to his house, which is under a much bigger mound, usually half-hidden under a bush.

He is a helpless little chap above ground, for he can only move clumsily when he is not digging, and although his forelegs and shoulders are tremendously strong, the rest of his body is so soft and unprotected that a gentle squeeze is enough to kill him.

Be kind to the little mole if you see him, for although he can spoil a garden lawn he doesn't do much harm elsewhere. His fur, of course, is very valuable, and that is why traps are set for him.

SNAKES

Most people have a horror of snakes, but there is no need to be afraid of them, and every reason to watch them, for they are fascinating creatures. There are only three kinds in this country, and the biggest and most common is the grass snake. You will most likely find him near water, because he lives on frogs and newts for choice. He can swim well, and climb, too, and sometimes when full grown is over three feet long. You will recognise him by his size, and by a yellow " collar " behind his head. Although he *looks* rather fierce, he is absolutely harmless, and cannot even bite. I have known some children who have tamed them and kept them as pets. The mother grass snake lays eggs in a rat hole or heaps of litter.

In some parts of southern England you may see another harmless snake called the smooth snake, but it is very rare now. It does not often grow to more than two feet.

The only other English snake is the adder or viper. This is quite different from the other two, both in appearance and habits, for it is short and rather thick in the body, with a short tail, and is rarely more than twenty inches long. Its head is flatter and broader, and you can always be sure of an adder by the black zigzag marking down the centre of its back. Adders love warmth and the sun, and are most likely to be found basking on a sunny bank or on some sandy heath amongst the heather. They are not fierce, and will only strike if attacked, but the adder's bite is very poisonous, and if you or one of your friends are ever bitten, suck the punctured skin hard and then spit out the venom and tie a handkerchief or a necktie tightly *above* the wound.

Baby adders break from their " eggs " almost as soon as they come from their mother's body, and they are then between six and eight inches long, and quite able to look after themselves. Many country people maintain that a mother adder when surprised with her babies on a sunny bank will open her mouth wide, and that the babies will jump down her throat to safety. I don't think the experts at the Zoo would admit this to be possible, but many people say that they have actually seen it happen.

Another country story is that a brew of ash leaves applied externally will cure an adder's bite.

* * *

BATS

The only *animal* with the power of true flight is the bat. I expect you have seen bats fluttering through the dusk and wondered at their strange, blundering flight, and perhaps been a little scared of them, too.

But the little bat is perfectly harmless and is a very wonderful animal, with gifts and characteristics difficult for us to understand. There are twelve different kinds in this country, but you are most likely to see the smallest, which is called the Common Bat, and which has a soft, reddish fur, with black ears and wings. These wings have no feathers but are a broad web of crinkled skin stretched over long, clawed fingers, rather in the way that the silk of an umbrella is stretched over its metal ribs. This skin is also joined to the hind legs and stretches nearly to the tip of its odd little tail. The body is rather like that of a mouse.

Although its flight is strangely silent it sometimes gives a shrill cry which is rather weird, but what is really uncanny about the bat is its skill in snatching from the air and *in the darkness* the flies and beetles upon which it lives. It hunts all through the night and is never seen on the wing in daylight, when it sleeps upside down by the hooks at the end of its " fingers " in an old barn or ruin, or even behind gutters and rain-pipes on the house.

If you watch the bat's crazy flight carefully you will notice that he never touches anything, even in the dark. Some wonderful sense tells him when an insect is near, and this in spite of the fact that his eyes are small and his sight poor, although he is *not* blind as some people say. It seems, therefore, that his hearing must be particularly keen and his wings so sensitive that they can " feel " something near them.

Woods and Forests

Loveliest of trees, the cherry now
Is hung with bloom along the bough,
And stands about the woodland ride
Wearing white for Eastertide.

Now, of my threescore years and ten,
Twenty will not come again,
And take from seventy springs a score,
It only leaves me fifty more.

And since to look at things in bloom
Fifty springs are little room,
About the woodlands I will go
To see the cherry hung with snow.

A. E. HOUSMAN

THIS is a poem worth remembering, because it expresses so many beautiful thoughts in so few words. A cherry tree " hung with blossom " is an unforgettable sight and, as the poet says, fifty springs cannot be enough to watch the wonder of things in bloom. Spring is something to welcome even in the city streets, but when she comes to a wood she comes with a magic that changes its appearance in a single night.

I think a wood is the most mysterious and exciting part of the countryside. When I was your age I used to be a little afraid to leave the sunshine of the open fields for the green gloom of the overhanging trees, but there were so many things to see and find and enjoy inside that I soon forgot my fears. I suppose that our awe of woods goes back to the days when our distant ancestors hunted through the forests that covered all our land; and, of course, in earliest pagan times, men worshipped trees. It is strange that woods should give such an impression of silence, because they are really so full of life—birds and squirrels in the trees ; rabbits, with stoats hunting them perhaps, on the ground ; hedgehogs in the ditches, mice in the banks, and maybe foxes and badgers waiting in their underground homes for the dusk.

But if you stand still and listen you will hear the gentle sounds of life around you. The sunlight is dappling the tangled undergrowth, and although the briars may seem to reach out to you as you begin to push past them up the little path, the wood is ready to share her secrets with you.

A wood is made up of trees, and trees give us wood, which we cannot do without. Wherever you are you can look round and see how much we rely upon wood in our daily lives, so you should know something about the kind of trees that grow in British woods and forests. There is not room here for pictures of all the trees you may find, but I hope I can tell you enough in a few pages to help you to recognise and remember most of them.

*   *   *

THE KING OF TREES

The oak is Britain's tree and the monarch of the forest. It is the one tree you are sure to recognise, with its great gnarled trunk and broad sweeping branches—and, of course, its acorns. We believe that the great forests which covered so much of England hundreds of years ago were oak, for they are trees which grow very slowly, and some of them still standing may well be over 1,000 years old. Ships of Britain's Navy were always built with oak until we used steel, and the wood is so hard when it is mature (at about 200 years old), that it has always been in demand for house beams, flooring, country gates and furniture. The lobed leaves of the oak are easy to recognise, and are like those of no other tree. At first they are a very pale green, but they soon get darker, and in autumn turn a rich golden brown.

*   *   *

THE ELM

The elm is probably the commonest tree in the country-side. There are several different kinds, but those most usually seen are the common elm and the wych elm, and they grow as often in the hedgerows and along the lanes as they do in the wood. Elms are easy to recognise because their big, heavy branches grow out from the trunk almost at right angles, quite near the ground, making a shady roof for the cattle and horses. The tree itself is usually very tall. The leaves are smallish and a darker green above than below, and set alternately on the stem. The leaves of the wych elm are larger than those of the common elm, which is not quite so spreading as its cousin. You cannot go far in the country without seeing elms. They are handsome, big trees and almost as impressive in winter as summer. The wood is valuable too, but is not very long lasting. It does not splinter, and is not affected much by the action of water, so it is often used for the piles of bridges and, at one time, pipes of elm were used to carry water.

But the elm is a dangerous tree, because its branches get blown down very easily, and it is not wise to shelter under it during a storm. Even in summer it has a habit of dropping one of its great branches without warning, and many farmers will tell you how they have lost cows and horses through the treachery of the elm.

* * *

THE BEECH

Unlike the elm, the beech is a forest tree, liking chalky soil best, and two or more are usually found growing near each other. It is a beautiful tree, and is most easily recognised by its silvery-grey, smooth bark. Sometimes its great branches sweep close down to the ground so that you can creep through them into a big, green tent carpeted with millions of the little fallen golden leaves and beech " mast " —the latter is the prickly container of the beech nuts which fall in the autumn. The nuts themselves are sweet and tasty, and much sought after by squirrels and badgers—and by some boys and girls! The nuts usually ripen and fill every fifth year; it used to be a country custom for the children of the village to make necklaces and bracelets by threading them together. The roots of the beech tree grow very near the surface, and you can often see them pushing out of the ground or reappearing a long way from the trunk. Beech wood is much used for furniture making.

* * *

THE QUEEN OF THE FOREST

If the oak is the king of the forest, surely the silver birch is his queen, for she is the daintiest and loveliest of all our trees. You will see her everywhere, for she grows as easily in a suburban garden as on the mountain-side. The bark is white and almost like paper—and indeed it has been proved that our ancestors used it *instead* of paper—and it peels off in strips from time to time, leaving the trunk striped with black bars like a zebra.

* * *

THE ASH

The ash is another beautiful tree, and a very useful one, too, because the timber is strong and can be steamed into many shapes ; it is used for the bodies of cars, for gliders and for aeroplanes. If you are a Boy Scout, your pole is almost certainly made from ash wood, and so are many walking-sticks. The tree is recognised by the smooth, grey trunk, but as it gets older the bark becomes furrowed. In the early spring the branches show their black sooty buds, which are arranged in pairs. The poet Tennyson described these in a way you will always remember when you see them —" *more black than ash buds in the front of March.*" In April and May, the buds break into yellow, purplish flowers, and later the female flowers which have been pollinated turn into the winged seeds which you can see twirling and spinning in the wind. The leaves appear late, and are made up of little leaflets arranged in spaces along the stalk.

* * *

THE CHESTNUT

Nearly everyone knows the " conker tree." Its proper name is the horse chestnut, and it is so called because there

59

is a mark like a horseshoe beneath each of the sticky buds, which are one of the earliest signs of spring. The big clusters of white or pink flowers stand up from among the leaves like candles on a Christmas tree. The horse chestnut is a big, handsome tree, but it is not often seen in forests or woods, because it did not originate in England, but was brought here in the sixteenth century from warmer lands.

I expect you know that conkers will grow if you plant them in the garden, or even in a narrow-necked vase full of water. A branch of the sticky buds picked off a chestnut tree will quickly open if you bring it indoors to a warm room, and place it in water.

The sweet chestnut, or Spanish chestnut, likes a warm climate, too, and is more generally found in the south. The nuts, as you know, are very nice to eat, although they do not ripen very well if the summer is cold and wet. This tree grows quickly and enjoys a splendid old age, and it is said that there are some in this country 2,000 years old. If you search the woods in autumn for the nuts you will have to get there before the squirrels, because they are particularly fond of eating and burying sweet chestnuts.

* * *

HAZELS AND HOLLIES

Not all woods are made up of big trees, and in many parts of the country you will find that it is broken up by coppices, which are little woods of low-growing trees. The commonest of these trees is the hazel, which grows strongly in bushy form, and gives golden catkins or " lamb's tails " in the spring, and tasty cob-nuts in the autumn. You cannot mistake the hazel with its pointed, rather heart-shaped little leaves.

Another tree which grows in the hedgerow as well as the coppice and wood is our old Christmas friend, the holly. An interesting fact about the holly is its defence against browsing animals when young. If you can find a little holly tree you will notice that *all* its leaves are hard and spiky because they are within reach of a hungry animal.

But as the tree gets older and grows taller, only the lower leaves retain their spikes, while the topmost branches, now out of reach of the marauders, grow leaves whose edges are smooth and harmless.

* * *

THE CONIFERS

The conifers are the pines, the firs and the larches—and all except the last are evergreens. There are many different kinds, but you will recognise them because they all bear needles and cones. A pine wood, with its thick carpet of brown needles and its lovely resinous smell, and with sunlight slanting down through the tall trunks, is a very lovely place. There is not much undergrowth in a pine wood—perhaps a little bracken or heather—and none under fir trees, as the thick carpet of needles prevents other things from growing. Actually all the trees in this family, except the Scots Pine, came from abroad, and perhaps that is why I am always reminded of Hansel and Gretel and of Grimm's Fairy Tales when I explore a pine wood. I used to imagine, too, that at any moment I should see the grey wolves slipping silently between the tree trunks, and if you went to Whipsnade Zoo before the war you could see wolves actually in such a pine wood.

All conifers like dry, sandy soil, and you often see them standing like lonely sentinels at the edge of a wild common or against the skyline of a distant hill. The Scots Pine is commonest, and may grow to a height of 100 feet. The bark is pinky brown in colour, and often the lower branches die and fall. Pitch and resin ooze from the trunk.

The firs include the Douglas Fir and the spruce, which is really our Christmas tree.

The larch is a dainty little tree and easily remembered, because it loses its leaves in the autumn and is almost the first to regrow them in the spring. These bright green leaves are unbelievably delicate and feathery. We get turpentine from the larch.

All the conifers grow quickly, and their timber is very

valuable, being used for scaffolding, railway sleepers, gates, fences, telegraph poles, pit props and boats. In Canada and Scandinavia spruce is pulped for paper-making.

* * *

THE SYCAMORE

The sycamore is sometimes found in woods, though more often in hedgerows, but as it grows nearly everywhere you are likely to know it by its smooth, grey bark and big leaves with five-pointed lobes. Often these leaves are spotted with a black fungus, but when they open in May they are pink rather than green. The seeds are carried by a little pair of wings.

ELDER, HAWTHORN AND ROWAN

There are some trees in our woods which are particularly noticeable because they carry lovely blossoms in summer and berries in the autumn. Commonest of these is the elder, which is a bushy, quick-growing tree bearing heavy clusters of creamy-white flowers which give off rather a sickly scent. In the early autumn the elder is loaded with ripe purple berries, which country people gather for home-made wine and jellies. Chickens like these ripe berries, too, and they are very good for them. The elder tree throws out many bright green shoots, which can be cleared of the soft pith inside and used as blow-pipes or pea-shooters or whistles.

Nearly every wood contains some hawthorn trees, which also grow in hedges and on commons and mountain-sides. The gnarled and twisted trunks give an impression of great age, but the branches grow thickly, and the lovely " May flowers " of white and pink are protected by sharp spikes. For this reason the hawthorn is a favourite nesting-place for birds. In the late autumn the tree is generally covered with a mass of clustered scarlet berries called " haws." It is said that, as with the holly, a heavy harvest of berries foretells a fierce winter. Some hawthorns hold their berries until deep into the winter, but birds are so fond of the fruit that they usually gobble it up greedily long before the weather becomes really hard.

Another gay and lovely tree is the rowan or mountain ash. This is a much taller tree than the elder or hawthorn, and its trunk is straight and smooth. The blossoms grow in white clusters, rather like those of the elder, and the ripe berries are a vivid scarlet. You can easily pick out the rowan rising above the other trees in a wood in the autumn. Many legends and stories have grown up round the rowan—some say that it is lucky, and others the opposite. It is to be found in some churchyards in Wales, and we are told that it was planted in these parts because it was considered sacred, and that on a certain day in each year every villager wore a cross made from the wood of the rowan tree.

* * *

FORESTER AND WOODMAN

Just as the farmer coaxes crops from the soil and raises stock for meat and hides and wool on his land, and is only successful when he is experienced and skilled, so there must be men equally skilled to tend the forest and cut the timber.

As, in this country, we have had to fight two great wars in twenty-five years, we have used up very great reserves of our own timber. Many magnificent forests and woods have been cut down, and we are using up timber more quickly than we can grow it. But in many parts of the British Isles you can see immense new forests planted out by hand and growing up for the use of generations still to come. Most of these forests are conifers, because they grow quickly.

Forestry is a very skilled craft, amd the men who make a livelihood amongst trees have hard and interesting work. A forester is a man who farms woods and makes a living by raising and selling timber. A woodman is a man who works for the forester, in the same way as a farm-hand works for a farmer. Forestry is an all-the-year-round job. There is a splendid book published which will tell you how the woodman's year is filled, and the name is given in the Book Section on page 137

If you are fascinated by woods and forests, it is interesting to know that woods must be kept clean and clear of undergrowth, and must be properly drained if the trees are to grow strong and healthy ; that the " nurseries " of little trees (all of which will have been grown from seed and probably transplanted several times) must be protected from rabbits, who can nibble hundreds of pounds' worth of damage in a night, and that all forests must be protected against fire in the dry months.

Fire was proving a grave menace before the war, when there were plenty of cars on the roads, and people were careless with cigarette ends or matches. If you are able to explore one of the forests of hand-planted trees, you will see that they are planted in straight or diagonal lines, and that at definite intervals the trees are intersected by straight, bare stretches of turf. These avenues are called " rides," and they act as fire breaks as well as roads down which the felled trees will be carried one day.

The danger of fire is perhaps not as great in the big "mixed " forests and woods which have been growing probably for over 1,000 years, because the trees themselves are too big to burn easily. But the dry undergrowth on the forest's floor is very inflammable—in March and April just as much as in the summer, unless the spring is very wet—and much damage can be done before help comes. In some countries, at certain seasons of the year, special fire watchers keep vigil on the top of tall towers so that they can watch high over the tree-tops for that tell-tale haze or smell of smoke that means danger and disaster to the forester.

*　　　*　　　*

Whenever you are in a wood you will be careful about fires, won't you ? Never light a fire in a wood if you can avoid it, but if you do, cover the hot ashes with earth before you leave. Sun shining on to a piece of broken glass has often started a serious fire, so don't leave broken bottles at your picnic place. Big brooms and spades are usually kept in forests in readiness for fire fighting, but if you ever see or smell the blue smoke of burning wood and cannot deal with the fire yourself, run for help as quickly as you can, being sure that you do not lose your sense of direction on the way.

Log Fires

Most country people burn wood in their open fires if they can, and a fire of coal and logs together is the most cheerful and comforting blaze in the world. But all woods burn in a different way, with varied-coloured flames and smells, and you may find it fun to try to recognise some of them.

The oak log is the best of all for an open fire, because it is so hard. It burns slowly, with bluish edges to the flames and with great heat. The conifers—larch, pine and fir— burn too readily, with a great fuss and noise. The resin in these logs makes them splutter and spark dangerously, and a fire heaped with pine logs should never be left, for it is certain to throw out sparks on to the hearthrug. The smell of burning pine, however, is lovely, as is the scent of apple, plum or cherry wood, though the latter burns through rather quickly. Beech and ash both burn beautifully—the former with a hot crimson flame and the latter brightly.

Trees which grow quickly always seem to burn quickly, and for this reason, willow, birch and poplar are not worth cutting up or buying. Hawthorn is so hard it will hardly burn at all, and horse chestnut is sulky and unsuitable.

THE BEECH AND THE OAK

For the slender beech and the sapling oak,
That grow by the shadowy rill,
You may cut down both at a single stroke,
You may cut down which you will.

But this you must know, that as long as they grow,
Whatever change may be,
You can never teach either oak or beech
To be aught but a greenwood tree.

THOMAS LOVE PEACOCK

GREEN RAIN

Into the scented woods we'll go
And see the blackthorn swim in snow.
High above, in the budding leaves,
A brooding dove awakes and grieves ;
The glades with mingled music stir,
And wildly laughs the woodpecker.
When blackthorn petals pearl the breeze,
There are the twisted hawthorn trees
Thick-set with buds, as clear and pale
As golden water or green hail—
As if a storm of rain had stood
Enchanted in the thorny wood,
And, hearing fairy voices call,
Hung poised, forgetting how to fall.

MARY WEBB

Birds

It is just possible to imagine the countryside without animals, because most of them are shy and rarely seen or heard, but everyone can realise that the country without birds would be a silent and cheerless place.

The life of a bird is one of Nature's greatest miracles, for of all living things God has granted to birds the most complete mastery of the air. Birds—with a very few exceptions—are our friends, for they guard the crops in our gardens, fields and orchards by destroying innumerable pests.

Folklore is rich with stories and legends of birds ; there is constant reference to them in the Bible, and for as long as man has been able to record his thoughts and emotions he has sung their praises. Birds are the gay heralds of the seasons, and many a man has been cheered by the cheeky chirrup of a sparrow in a city street and the friendliness of the brave robin on a grey winter day.

For some years before the war more and more grown-ups were adopting the hobby of watching birds, and so learning something of their industry, courage and patience, and the beauty of their flight, plumage and song. I cannot suggest any better hobby than this for a boy or girl on holiday in the spring. Once you have discovered for yourself the excitement of watching a pair of birds build their nest, and then rear their family, every country walk will be an adventure.

There are hundreds of wild birds in the British Isles, and I cannot do more here than give you a few notes about some of them, in the hope that they will help you to recognise the commonest and those which are perhaps not so often seen, but about which you have often read.

* * *

NESTS

Have you ever realised what a stupendous task is undertaken each spring by two frail birds when they build an entirely new home? The houses in which we live last our lifetime and longer, and are built by other people for us. But most birds make a· new house every year, and each nest is a miracle of artistry and engineering skill. Every blade of grass, every twig, every wisp of hay or straw is carried and put into the correct place with the bird's beak. He has no other tools. The site is chosen first and then both birds set to work in a fury of industry.

If you can find a quiet spot near a puddle or a stream you can see them at work, for they use mud to cement the woven strands together, and if you watch carefully you will see that each scrap of hay or grass or twig is tried with their beaks before they fly away with it. This is because they must be positive that it can be *bent* easily to shape.

Each bird builds its nest in a particular way and in a particular place. The thrush, for instance, will never build under the eaves, but in a hedge or the fork of a tree. Robins build in all sorts of odd places, and do not mind being near the house. Once building begins, both cock and hen work with tremendous energy, and often by the end of the first day the skeleton of the new house is complete. Sometimes a nest is ready for occupation within a week, but the time of building depends upon how far the builders have to fly for their materials.

It is a very wonderful thing that different birds lay eggs of different colours and that eggs laid in nests on the ground are " camouflaged " to the colour of their surroundings, and eggs laid in trees or hedges are often gaily and beautifully coloured. Once the eggs are laid, however, the parents never leave them until they are hatched. Some mothers are astonishingly courageous—robins, blackbirds and thrushes in particular—and refuse to leave their eggs even if you stand over them. When the eggs are hatched both cock and hen are kept busy feeding the babies, whose open beaks gape all day long for the titbits popped into their mouths by their tireless parents.

Later comes the first flying lesson, when the timid youngsters are pushed out of the safety of the nest and *made* to fly. In this the mother will prove quite ruthless. She knows that her babies are now ready to fly, and that a good mother sometimes seems to be hard and unrelenting. And, like all good mothers, she is right. Once the babies are in the air they must fly or fall. So they fly!

Most boys and girls enjoy collecting birds' eggs and learning to distinguish the different varieties, but there is a way to do this without robbing those carefully made nests of their precious contents. It is by making a Birds'-nest Map.

How to Make a Birds'-nest Map

If you are doing your bird-watching from a farm, it is easier to make a map of the surroundings than if you are exploring a different part of the countryside each day, with a village as a centre, but the best way of setting about it is to choose a fairly small district as a start, and make a simple sketch-map of it. Then, as you begin to find nests, mark them in on the map with a cross. Perhaps you could experiment with coloured inks, if you can get them, and use different colours for different birds. You are sure to find plenty of sparrows, thrushes and blackbirds' nests in the hedges round the farm, and your map will soon show where these are to be found. With the map it is fun to keep a " log book," in which you will record everything that you see as nesting progresses and the eggs are laid. You will probably want the following particulars :

Date when found. Location. Name of bird. State of nest (i.e. whether finished or in course of building). Number of eggs, and when laid. Description—that is, approximate size, colour, markings and so on. Date when hatched. Date when fledglings taught to fly. Date when nest left. Then you had better leave another space for notes in case you see anything else that is worth recording, and in a few weeks' time you will have a splendid record of the bird life of the district. If you have a camera, the book could, of course, be illustrated with your own pictures.

MIGRATION

To migrate means to move from one place to another, and one of the greatest and most inexplicable wonders of Nature is the migration of certain birds as the seasons change. So before I give you some notes about the different types of birds seen in this country, you should know something of this great mystery.

A number of our birds are only visitors, for they do not come until the spring, and they fly away again before the winter comes. The commonest of such visitors is the swallow, and we know a little more about his adventures perhaps than those of any other migrating bird. In some parts of the country you may see the first swallow by the end of March, and before April is out most of them have arrived.

We know that swallows cannot face the cold, and it must be for that reason that they leave us in the autumn. It has been proved by marking the birds (usually done by a tiny aluminium ring on the leg) that some actually fly 6,000 miles from Britain to South Africa. If they are only in search of warmth, we wonder why they do not stop in North Africa, which is warm enough, instead of flying over a continent. There is no answer to this. We do not know. Another extraordinary thing is that when all the other birds in South Africa are building nests and laying their eggs, the swallow leaves the sunshine she loves and flies back to England to lay her eggs, often in the very same nest under a cottage thatch that she used a year ago.

Nobody can understand this miracle or knows how swallows find their way these incredible distances. They are birds who never know a winter, and yet who have the strength to battle through wind and rain and over desert, swamp and forest twice a year. As July deepens into August swallows show a strange restlessness and collect in great flocks ready for the flight southwards. At some unspoken signal they say " Goodbye," and, straight as the flight of an arrow, speed away to the land they left only a few months before. If a baby swallow were put into a cage before he had learned to fly, this same strange power would cause him, when the time came, to beat himself to death against the bars in his efforts to go with the others.

And so, while summer lasts, our friend the swallow flashes and dips and turns round the house catching his insects, and then one morning we realise that he has gone and that summer has gone with him.

In some parts of Britain, in the spring, you can actually see the swallows arriving in large flocks. Day after day they come—some still flying tirelessly and some dropping from exhaustion.

Sometimes it happens that our weather is too severe for them when they do arrive, and then they have been known to come even into houses in search of warmth. They cannot survive the cold, so look out for them in the spring, and if the weather is bitter you may find one or two of these gallant little adventurers under the hedgerows dying for need of the sun they love. We welcome them because when we see them first we know that summer is just behind them.

* * *

THE OWL

When cats run home and light is come,
And dew is cold upon the ground,
And the far-off stream is dumb,
And the whirring sail goes round,
And the whirring sail goes round ;
Alone and warming his five wits,
The white owl in the belfry sits.

When merry milkmaids click the latch,
And rarely smells the new-mown hay,
And the cock hath sung beneath the thatch
Twice or thrice his roundelay,
Twice or thrice his roundelay ;
Alone and warming his five wits,
The white owl in the belfry sits.

ALFRED TENNYSON

I am going to tell you first about the owl—not because

he is the commonest of British birds—but because such a lot has been written about him. There are five different kinds of owl to be found in these islands, but the most common are the barn owl and the tawny or wood owl.

Tennyson was referring to the barn owl when he wrote the poem quoted overleaf, but he was not correct when he called him white. He *looks* to be all white when he is flying and seen from below, but his back and the upper sides of his wings are sandy and grey. But it is true that he sits in the belfry, for he likes to find an old ruin or tower for his home, and, as his name suggests, is very fond of barns. The poet's reference to the " whirring sail " is, if you haven't guessed it already, a windmill, for the owl lives almost entirely on mice and rats, and, as you know, these are to be found where the grain is stored.

Because the owl looks grave and solemn he has always been taken as the symbol of wisdom, and the dark circles of feathers round his eyes do give the impression of spectacles. I expect you have heard the expression " wise as an owl."

There are a lot of silly legends about him, the most common of which is that his weird and haunting cry is the forerunner of evil, and that it is unlucky to hear his rather frightening, ugly screech. The barn owl is *not* the bird who cries " Tu-whit, Tu-whoo." That is his cousin, the tawny or wood owl, who lives in the woods and does not like ruins. You can tell the two apart easily enough, because " tawny " has no white about him, and his plumage is nut-brown, often barred with darker stripes.

The other three owls are not so common. There is the little owl, which is an extremely fierce fighter and a comparative newcomer, and her short-eared and long-eared cousins.

All owls sleep during the daylight, and as their eyes can only see properly in the dark they are rather helpless before then. They sleep " with one eye open," sitting upright, but just as soon as the light begins to fail you can see them drifting silently over the fields looking for mice. Sometimes the owl will eat fledglings and small birds, who are terrified of him, but if ever he is foolish enough to venture out in the daylight, which dazzles him, he is liable to be fiercely attacked by sparrows, robins, or wrens, who will mob him unmercifully. But in the dark he is a terror and a scourge, for his eyes are so powerful and he is such a savage hunter that no animal is safe from him.

You may surprise him on his perch in the barn or in the wood in the daytime, but you are more likely to see him in the evening or on a moonlight night as he goes hunting.

Owls are bad nest builders, for they only scrape together a few feathers and dust in which to lay their eggs ; but you can look for these in ruins, or in barns or in the woods, and especially in hollow trees. The long-eared owl uses the old nest of a pigeon, hawk or crow.

> *Save that from yonder ivy-mantled tow'r*
> *The moping owl does to the moon complain.*

THOMAS GRAY

* * *

THE WREN

The wren is one of our smallest birds and also one of the cheekiest. You will recognise him—or her, I suppose, because she is generally known as Jenny or Kitty Wren—easily enough by her rich, red-brown plumage, and her tip-tilted tail. Her song is clear and sweet and very loud for so small a bird. She also has a rather unusual habit of flying very low and creeping like a mouse through the undergrowth or hedges.

There are many legends told about the wren, some of which claim that he is the King of the Birds, and it does seem rather odd that such a lot of superstition should have grown up round such an insignificant-looking little bird.

Here is one of the stories that have come down from many generations, and that you will still hear in certain parts of the country to-day. Once upon a time all the birds met to choose their king, and because they were the wisest, the owls decided that the bird who could fly the highest should be accepted by them all as their sovereign. Bird after bird tried in vain to reach the eagle, but the wren had hidden himself on the eagle's back, and when the big bird could fly no higher, the wren jumped off and flew a few feet higher still, before settling down again amongst the eagle's feathers. When the two birds came back to earth the wren claimed to have flown the highest, and the eagle, although very angry, was too proud to answer so insolent a claim. After solemn consultation the owls decided that the wren did *not* fly the highest and that the eagle was king.

So then the little wren crept away in shame, and ever since that day, because he is so tiny, he does not attempt what he cannot do, and flies always close to the ground.

Now you will remember this story every time you see the little wren darting quickly to and fro around the garden, or down the hedgerows. It is, of course, only a coincidence that although the owl gave judgment against the wren in this story, wrens have been known to band together and attack an owl fiercely in daylight, and drive him before them in terror. This is to some extent because owls are nearly helpless in a bright light, but it is a fact that small birds do unite to mob him. Shakespeare knew this, too, for in *Macbeth* we read :

> for the poor wren,
> The most diminutive of birds, will fight,—
> Her young ones in her nest—against the owl.

The wren builds a most beautiful nest of moss, leaves, grass, feathers and wool, with a domed roof, and a little round door at the side, and generally chooses a hedge or a woodpile, but sometimes will build in a branch or in a hole in an old wall. The eggs are white and faintly speckled with red.

* * *

THE HOUSE SPARROW

Another small but courageous bird is the house sparrow, who is probably the commonest of all British birds. He seems to be able to live and breed as successfully in the city as in the country, where he really belongs, and wherever we go the sparrow seems to be with us.

The sparrow is really rather a nuisance because, although he seems to be able to live on anything and change his diet as it suits him, he is a great spoiler of gardens and a robber of grain. It is true that in summer he eats caterpillars and insects, and feeds his young on them, too, but every farmer's hand is against him, and it is not surprising that he is suspicious and watchful of human beings.

Sparrows are great talkers ! Except when they are building their nests, they seem to go about in gangs, and are always arguing, chattering and fighting among themselves. They love dust baths, and it doesn't take them long to spoil a newly-sown seed bed if the soil is dry. They will build their nests nearly anywhere, just as long as it is near that of another sparrow and near a house. Under eaves and gutters, in the roof of the barn and in a creeper against a wall are favourite places. The eggs are grey or brown, covered with speckles and blotches. The cock sparrow has a smart black " bib " and white underparts, while the hen is all brown.

The house sparrow is not to be confused with the hedge sparrow, who is really misnamed, because he is no relation. The eggs of the latter, who does *not* nest near houses, are a lovely turquoise blue, and both male and female are a quiet, red-brown colour.

* * *

THE STARLING

The starling is not a likeable bird, but he has some remarkable habits. In appearance he is nearly black, but his feathers are glossy with purple and green in the spring, and he is thus rather handsome. If you are not careful you may confuse him at first sight with the blackbird, because both will be busy on the lawn in the early morning pulling worms out of the ground and looking for snails. But the blackbird's bill is bright orange, and he moves in long, springy hops, while the starling runs.

The starling is greedy and quarrelsome and extremely fond of company. You will hardly ever see him alone. In the garden he may have only one or two friends with him, but often they feed in hundreds and fly off in large flocks in the dawn to hunt for food. The starling likes grain, but some farmers refrain from shooting him because he does eat enormous quantities of beetles, caterpillars and harmful insects.

Starlings enjoy water, and you can often see a number of them taking a bath in a puddle or stream. They do not seem to have a song of their own, but they are certainly good mimics of others, and sometimes you can catch a starling sitting on a wall or a chimney-pot whistling like a blackbird.

The most interesting thing about the starling is his sociability and his amazing antics with his fellows in the evening. You may have seen these astonishing congregations of starlings wheeling and turning in the air as if in answer to a hidden commander, all wheeling and turning and dipping at the same time in the same way.

Flocks of starlings come for miles to roost in the same place every night, and the smaller flocks join up with others as they fly, until sometimes the sky is black with beating wings. Nobody knows why this is done, but it does seem as if they obey some unknown power or instinct as they make their way " home." Night after night the flocks come back to the same place, and even after they seem to have settled, they will suddenly, at some mysterious signal, wheel into the evening sky again, setting up a tremendous clamour. I have known a flock of starlings chatter and squabble for at least an hour before settling down to sleep.

The starling's eggs are a pale greenish-blue, and they are laid in a nest in a hole in a tree or a space in a wall or a barn. Sometimes you may find single eggs dropped unbroken on the lawn.

* * *

ROOKS

Another very sociable bird is the **rook, the largest** of our common birds. Rooks not only like each other's company, for they never nest alone, but they seem to like humans, too ; their colonies are nearly always near houses or farms. The rook is a big bird—over twice the size of a starling and almost jet black, with a wide wing span—and you cannot mistake him as he circles round the rookery in the tree tops, calling and being answered by his friends with hoarse " caws."

No other land birds have quite the same interesting habits as rooks, the most important of which is their astonishing ability to live and work, hunt and breed together, almost in the way in which human beings do. They actually build their own towns, for a rookery may contain as many as a thousand nests. If you are able to discover a rookery near you, probably at the top of a high tree, and should come back to it in forty years' time, you might well find that it is still being used.

When the baby rooks have been pushed from the nest and have learned to depend upon themselves, the parents desert the rookery. This usually happens in May, or at the beginning of June. But the fledglings seem to stay with the parents after that, feeding with them in the fields and going back with them to the roosting-place at night. Their roosting-places are almost as remarkable as the rookeries, for the birds join up with several other colonies, and all roost together in big trees, which may be a long way from the nests they have now deserted. This goes on all through the winter, and many thousands of rooks—and jackdaws, crows and magpies sometimes—return to the same place every night.

But the odd thing is that rooks never seem to forget their nests, and sometimes, in the winter, they will return and look at them. Then, in February, they start to repair the old nests and sometimes to build new ones, and one day you may find that they are all back again—all quarrelling and playing together. They are extremely noisy birds, and some people say that they have a language of their own. Certainly their vocabulary is varied, and they seem to understand each other.

The nests are always built in the highest possible tree, and are generally found in elms. The nest is an untidy-looking structure of loose sticks, lined with grass or hair. The eggs are greenish with brown speckles.

*　　*　　*

MAGPIES

The magpie belongs to the same family as the rook. He is a real character, and probably the greatest chatterbox of all our birds. He is handsome—black and white—with a very long tail and quick-beating wings. The nest is generally built in a big tree, and has a roof and a rounded entrance at the side, with sharp thorns pointing outwards to protect it. It is a very fine nest, and there is a story about it that you may like to remember.

As you know, nearly every other bird's nest is open to the sky, and once, long ago, all the birds met together to talk about nest-building, because none of them was particularly successful. After a lot of talk, the owl advised them all to ask the magpie how he managed to make so splendid a nest. The magpie was quite willing.

" First I take two sticks and lay one across the other, so . . ."

" But we know that already," all the birds interrupted rudely.

The magpie was naturally annoyed, but went on patiently :

" Then you must find some moss and be ready with plenty of leaves and mud . . ."

But again the birds interrupted rudely and shouted that they knew all that and had done that already.

Once again the magpie, although extremely angry, started to explain, but the other birds were stupid and would not listen to him, so he asked them why they had come to him, if they did not want to learn, and sent them away. And to this day none of them know how to make a snug roof over their nests like the magpie's.

Magpies can be tamed and taught to speak a few human words. Like the jackdaw and other members of that family, they have a weakness for anything bright and sparkling, and will often steal rings or jewellery, or shining pieces of tin, and carry them away to the nest.

* * *

JACKDAWS

The jackdaw is also a member of the rook family and is rather like him, but for a grey patch on the back of the head and neck. He is much smaller, though, and his wing-beats are even quicker. He also likes to build in company and often chooses old ruins, a church tower, or the edge of a cliff, in which to set up a colony. Occasionally he nests in trees, and the eggs have a bluish tinge and are spotted with brown.

There is an old country saying that if jackdaws are seen coming home to their nests or to their roosting-places later than usual, or even if they are seen much alone, then cold or bad weather is on the way.

* * *

THE CUCKOO

Some people like the cry of the cuckoo because they say it is a sign that summer is just round the corner, and this is true enough. But whether or no humans like his cry, it is certain that all other birds dislike him, and will sometimes attack him fiercely.

There is every good reason for their dislike, for the cuckoo's habits make him an outlaw. He comes to us from the sunnier south in the spring, and leaves us again in August. Instead of building a nest for herself, the hen cuckoo watches what other birds are doing, and searches for their nests— of the meadow-pipit or the pied wagtail in particular—but if she cannot find these two favourites of hers, she will lay her egg in other nests. She lays only one egg in any one nest and sometimes, if the nest has a side entrance, she will lay the egg on the ground, and then carry it up in her beak, and push it through the narrow opening into the nest.

When the baby cuckoo is hatched, it instinctively pushes any other eggs or baby fledglings out of the nest. The curious fact about this is that the young cuckoo does not grow feathers quickly, and is hatched with a hollow in his back, which enables him to push everything and everybody out of the nest on to the ground. Another odd thing is that the foster parents do not seem to object to this brutality, and make tremendous efforts to feed this quaint foster-baby, until in a few short weeks he has outgrown the nest, and them, too.

So you see that although the cuckoo may be a sentimental herald of spring, he is responsible for the death of many small birds who are our valued friends. There is no mistaking the cuckoo, for, apart from his cry, he is a big grey bird with spots of white in his tail. The white underparts are barred with dark-grey stripes and his wing-beat is slow as he flaps out of the tree at the edge of the wood.

Sometimes the female cuckoo lays eggs of a different colour, to match those of the bird whose nest she has selected for her piracy.

*   *   *

TWO SONGSTERS

The nightingale and the skylark are both famed for the beauty of their song.

Hark ! hark ! the lark at Heaven's gate sings,

wrote Shakespeare, and it is true that this little brown bird seems to spend all his time circling higher and yet higher into the blue sky of a summer's day, trilling his sweet song of joy. He starts before the sun is over the horizon, and flies up into the dawn to greet it. Often he soars so high that he is lost to sight, but when he comes down he is still singing. If he sees you, he will alight some distance from his nest, which is usually under a tuft of grass or in the hollow made by a horse's hoof, and then run to it along the ground so that you have no clue to its position.

As May lengthens into June so does the little skylark sing more joyously, for he seems to worship the sun and gives thanks for being alive. He seems to be always either on the ground or in the air, for he is rarely seen in a tree or bush,

Mother Swan and her baby cygnet on their nest beside the water. Mother is snow white, of course, but did you know her baby is grey at first?

1.

2.

5.

1. *Barn Owl comes out at night for his food.* 2. *Song Thrush and family.* 3. *The handsome Jay with hungry mouths to feed.* 4. *The " cooing " Wood Pigeon ; enemy of farmer and gardener, as he eats their plants.* 5. *Jackdaw and young — also hungry.*

6. *The greedy Cuckoo fledgling fed by its kind fostermother, the Meadow Pipit.* 7. *The gaily-coloured Kingfisher who nests in the river bank (note the fish in his beak).*

8. *Great Tit at the entrance to his nesting hole with a " titbit " for the family.*

3.

4.

6.

7.

9. *The frail Reed Warbler and
its wonderful little nest in the reeds.*

10. *The Skylark builds her nest on the
ground.*

Two enemies of the farmer : the dainty Field Mouse (left) balanced on a swaying stalk, and the innocent-looking rabbit (bottom left).

The Hedgehog (top picture) eats snails and grubs and lives in hedgerows and ditches ; he sleeps all the winter. Stoat (above) and Weasel (below)·

but you will recognise him by his mottled brown body and yellowish, spotted breast. He has a little brown crest on his head, which he can lower if he wishes. The eggs are thickly speckled with brown.

Whereas the lark sings to the sun, the nightingale sings to the moon. No other bird sings so sweetly, and although he can sometimes be heard in the daytime, it is in the stillness of a moonlit night that his incomparable song is most easily recognised. It is difficult to describe, but once you have heard it you will never forget its lovely, loud, full, deep notes, and beautiful trills and warbles. It is amazing that such an insignificant little brown bird can produce a song that has inspired poets throughout the ages. He is one of our summer visitors, and is not with us long, and he sings at his best soon after his arrival, half-way through April until the end of June, when the olive-brown eggs are hatched. The nest is built on or just above the ground, generally in the shelter of a bush.

If you can get permission to go out into the wood one still night in May, the best time to hear the nightingale is about two hours after sunset.

*　　　*　　　*

THE BLACKBIRD

It is time I reminded you of the blackbird, with his yellow bill and glossy jet-black coat. A very smart and confident gentleman is the blackbird, with his rich, clear voice which you can hear—if you are awake—before the sun is up. The hen blackbird is rather dowdy in comparison with her mate, because she is a dull brown and has no yellow bill. But she is an extremely brave mother, and I have often walked right up to her on her nest, while she watched me courageously, but sat firmly on her eggs. Blackbirds are fond parents and fine nest-builders, choosing a hedge or an evergreen bush for their home. You can recognise the nest because it is smoothly lined with mud, and then lined again with grass and horsehair. The eggs are greenish-blue speckled with brown, and several families are raised each year.

The Song Thrush

The song thrush is as well known in our gardens and hedgerows as the blackbird, and has many of the same habits. He, too, is a beautiful and welcome singer, and he, too, hunts over the lawn to catch the early worm. He likes snails very much, and sometimes you can see him carry one to a flat stone which he uses as an anvil until the shell is broken.

The nest is built fairly near the ground in a hedge, in a fork of a tree, or in the ivy against a wall, and you might mistake it for a blackbird's but for the eggs, which are an exquisite turquoise blue, spotted with black. You will know the song thrush by his brown plumage and light, speckled breast.

* * *

The Lapwing

One of our most useful and unusual-looking birds is the lapwing, which is sometimes called the peewit or green plover. He is a wild, shy bird, who seems to love lonely places, for he is often seen on moors, marshes and tidal mud flats. But in winter and early spring you can often see lapwings in hundreds, wheeling and turning in their strange, clumsy flight over the newly-ploughed fields, calling their plaintive " Pee-wit, Pee-wit."

The farmer welcomes the lapwing because he eats wireworms, leatherjackets, snails, slugs and worms, and he is a very handsome fellow when he is on the ground, for his plumage is green and red and white, and he has a graceful tuft or crest on his head.

Although lapwings are shy of men, they like each other's company, and you are not likely to see them flying alone or in pairs even in the breeding season.

The dark, green-brown blotched eggs are laid in a rough nest in a hollow in the ground, and are so coloured that they are difficult to see. If you come too near, the parents become frantic with anxiety, and will do almost anything to lead you away from the nest. A peewit has been known to pretend to have a broken wing by dragging it helplessly over the ground and crying piteously.

The Hawk

There are still a few birds of prey in these islands, but the two you are most likely to see are the sparrow hawk and the kestrel. The latter is the commoner, and he is recognised by the way in which he hovers over his tiny prey in the fields beneath him. He flies fast and quite low, and then suddenly stops dead, remaining motionless, with wingtips only beating the air. Then he will swoop on the mouse below, which would probably have been invisible to us even if we stood just above him. Most farmers welcome kestrels because, with stoats and weasels, they are the greatest enemies of mice, who can eat and destroy tons of grain in the stacks before it is threshed.

* * *

The Finches

I wish I had room to tell you all about the jolly finches in their gay plumage and with their cheerful songs. They are a happy family—the house sparrow is a close relation—and they all have short, strong curved beaks so shaped that they can easily pull up and eat grain and seeds. In the summer they eat insects.

Those you are most likely to see are the chaffinch, the greenfinch, the bullfinch and the goldfinch. The goldfinch is perhaps the loveliest of them all, and is now increasing in numbers. For a time it was a popular cage bird, but fortunately it is now protected by law, and so the cruelty of caging another wild bird has been checked.

* * *

The Tits or Titmice

The tits are unlike other birds because they are such clever acrobats. The great tit and the cheeky little blue tit are the commonest, and they are the only British birds who hang upside down on twigs in search of insects, and who will perform the same trick on the hanging half of a coconut, a piece of fat, or a string of monkey nuts outside our windows. They love fat and will pick a bone dry in no time. Another name for the blue tit is the Tom tit.

Other members of the family are the coal-titmouse, Marsh-titmouse and long-tailed titmouse.

*　　　*　　　*

There are many more birds to watch and learn about than I have been able to introduce to you here, but I have told you a little about those you are most likely to see. There still remain two I want to mention—the first a mischievous nuisance, and the second the friendliest of all birds.

THE WOOD PIGEON

It is easy to think of the pretty ring-dove or wood pigeon with his soft " coo-coooo-e-coo-cuk " as a gentle, inoffensive bird who calls soothingly in the summer from the tree tops. He is *not* an inoffensive bird ! With the rabbit and the rat he is one of the great agricultural pests of to-day, and as he seems to be increasing, he is a very great menace to the farmer, the gardener and the allotment holder.

If you look at him closely you will see a red, ugly eye and a cruel curved beak. With this beak he will destroy months of work in a few minutes, for he takes particular pleasure in ripping green vegetables to shreds. He seems to like all growing crops, but he is specially fond of the scarce, winter-growing cabbages and of grain. Although he is a greedy eater, when he finds a field or garden full of greens, he seems to go off to fetch all his friends and relations, who set to work with a will and help him to destroy everything that is growing.

Most farmers and gardeners would thank you if you destroyed the glossy white eggs which the wood pigeon lays in the untidy nest in the tree tops.

*　　　*　　　*

ROBIN REDBREAST

> *Art thou the bird whom man loves best,*
> *The pious bird with the scarlet breast,*
> *Our little English robin ?*

WILLIAM WORDSWORTH.

Our robin is perhaps the most loved and most typical of

all British birds. He is gay ; he is bold ; he is independent yet friendly, and he reminds us of Christmas and of home. Unlike the rooks and the starlings, he hates crowds and prefers his own company. He is a great fighter, and will allow no other bird into the particular little part of the hedgerow or garden which he has made his own. He does not seem to want to go far afield, like many other birds, to find his food, but sets up a kingdom of his own and appoints himself the sole ruler.

You will have noticed that he is not at all afraid of humans, but does, in fact, like to attract their attention, either by his glorious song or by flying round them and following them. We have a robin in our garden who seems to know when I fetch the spade from the tool shed. He stands, with his head on one side, a few feet from my boots as I dig, waiting for me to turn up a worm, and when I stick the spade in the ground for a few minutes' rest, he flies up and perches on the handle and watches me with his bright black eyes.

The robin is intensely jealous and will instantly attack any other small bird with red feathers—and regrettable though it is—he even fights his wife and his children when the time comes for them to leave him undisputed king of his own kingdom ! This is because robins eat worms, insects and other tiny living things, and these are difficult to find in the winter. If several robins are sharing the same kingdom, they may all starve, but if each king or queen sticks to his or her own " country," each stands a better chance of living through the winter.

Robins build beautiful little nests, generally in a hole in a tree, a wall or bank. Sometimes, though, they build in the oddest places, such as an old tin or kettle which has been thrown away, or in an old hat, or in a barn. The eggs are white, faintly speckled with red.

There are many legends and superstitions about the robin, and it has always been considered unlucky to destroy his nest or his babies. Do you know the story of how he got his red breast ? Once he was a little brown bird—as indeed his babies are now—but when Our Lord was wearing His crown of thorns Robin was so overcome with sorrow and sympathy for His suffering, that he flew up and tried to pluck the sharp spikes aside to relieve the pain. For this act of kindness the little brown robin's breast has ever since been stained as red as the blood which flowed from Our Lord's forehead, so that we may all be reminded that He suffered and died for us.

If you watch the robin's behaviour, you will soon see that he does act as if he were specially privileged, and he wants you to know it, too.

> *A robin redbreast in a cage*
> *Puts all Heaven in a rage.*

WILLIAM BLAKE.

Flowers

. . . daffodils,
That come before the swallow dares, and take
The winds of March with beauty ;

SHAKESPEARE wrote those lovely words. When you are old enough to read what he wrote for yourself, you will realise how the greatest of all English writers loved and understood the English countryside and the men and women who lived and worked in it.

Birds and flowers mark the seasons ; but even before the first feathered herald of the new year has piped to us, a few frail flowers have braved the snow and cheerless gloom of winter. Flowers are Nature's gayest and loveliest adornment and those that grow in fields and woods and hedges are the first relations of all those which grow in our gardens—although of course, some of the garden ones grow wild in foreign countries, and have been brought over and cultivated here.

Except on the very gloomiest and shortest days, you will find wild flowers in the countryside, and although there are many hundreds of different specimens in these islands, it is great fun to know how to recognise them and to learn something of the various families to which they belong.

Flowers belong to different families, just as birds do, but there is not room here to tell you about them, although there are plenty of clever books that do. Just as some families of birds thrive on mountain-sides and some in the hedgerows, so you will find the different flower families on different soils and in different places. Some, for instance, grow well on chalk and are never seen on grassy commons ; kingcups like the wet and anemones generally like the shade of a wood or copse.

Flowers in their natural state look so beautiful that we are nearly always tempted to pick some and take them home. Pick them, by all means, if you are neither destructive nor greedy. It is silly to pick more than you need and throw some away to die. It is stupid and thoughtless to pull wild flowers up by the roots. If everybody did that, the country-side would very soon become bare and empty of the flowers we all enjoy so much.

Because I can only remind you here of a few of the British wild flowers I suggest we go for a walk together down the lane, over the fields, and into the wood and see what we shall find. I shall have to cheat a little, because not all the flowers I mention would actually be blooming at the same time—we should not see the vivid, scarlet poppy in the fields, for instance, on the same day in which the gentle, frail anemone drooped her head in the hazel copse. But I promise that between March and August you would have a good chance of seeing all these flowers.

Now let us start. Bring a notebook if you like, so that you may keep a record of where you find each flower growing. We go down the lane which runs between high thorn hedges with a ditch of running water on the left-hand side.

* * *

THE CELANDINE

On the very first day when it is possible to imagine that spring is just round the corner—it may be as early as February —you will see the dainty celandine on the banks of the lane or the edge of the ditch. Its little golden, starlike petals are quite unmistakable and, although it is one of the commonest of the wayside flowers, we might well start our collection with it. The leaves are sometimes marked with white patches and, oddly enough, they vary a lot in shape and size, but they are generally heartshaped. Don't confuse the celandine with the buttercup, with its longer stalk, rounded petals and cuplike shape.

COW PARSNIP

Later in the year, from June to September, the hedgerows of our lane are likely to be thick with the tall, coarse-growing cow parsnip. The plant grows as high as six feet, and it has a thick, hairy, hollow stem from which branch stalks bearing large leaves and the flat heads of bloom. These blooms consist of hundreds of minute flowers at the end of short stalks branching out, like the ribs of an umbrella, from the main stems. Another name for this flower is hog-weed.

* * *

HONEYSUCKLE

Sometimes, on a warm sunny evening in June when the bees are droning sleepily down the hedgerows, there may come to you on the breeze the strong, sweet, heady smell of honeysuckle (or woodbine) in bloom. The honeysuckle is a climber with a rough, tough stem, and the creamy pink and yellow " tongued " flowers may be difficult to pick, high among the thorns of the hedge. You cannot possibly mistake the honeysuckle for anything else, though, and it always twines from left to right.

* * *

ARUMS

In the long grass above the ditch, in April, you may easily discover the odd-looking arums, which are called by several names by the country people—Cuckoo-pint, Lords-and-Ladies, and Jack-in-the-Pulpit. I like the last two names best and can quite understand how they were chosen, for the " flower "—which is not really the flower—is a spike standing erect inside a green hood. The dark spikes are the lords and the pale spikes are the ladies, and the flowers are clustered at the bottom of the spike, which is a device to attract insects. The leaves are dark green and often blotched with purple stains. Later in the year the hood disappears and the female flowers become a bunch of juicy, bright scarlet berries, which should not be touched because they are poisonous.

HAREBELL

The dainty little harebell, which you are as likely to see on the banks of the lane as you are on the common, belongs to the family called by the Latin name *Campanulaceæ*. This is easy to remember because the word means " Little bell," and that describes the harebell precisely. It is so dainty and of such an exquisite blue that it is easy to understand why it has been described as a Fairy flower. The tiny blooms, in late summer, all hang downwards from the thin stalks as if a touch would be enough to set them tinkling. This is the true bluebell of Scotland, but it is no relation to the so-called bluebell which grows in our woods and has a long, fleshy stalk. The harebell fades quickly when picked.

* * *

RAGGED ROBIN

Poor Ragged Robin ! He does look rather tattered and torn, and he's nearly all legs. You will find him where the soil is damp and he likes a wet meadow or a ditch, and flowers between May and August. He grows to about two feet and sometimes his stem is pinkish and inclined to be sticky. The leaves are slender and narrow ; the feathery-looking flowers are pink, and their shaggy appearance is due to the fact that each rosy petal is cut into four narrow segments—two short and two long. He is a near relation to another common flower called the red campion.

* * *

RED CAMPION

The red campion is certain to be growing in the hedge banks, for it likes the damp, and the flowers can be found from June to October, or even November, if the autumn is mild. The stem grows quite high and is slender, grasslike and jointed, and the flowers are a lovely rose-pink. The leaves grow in pairs from the joints in the stalk.

WHITE CAMPION

This is sometimes called bladder campion. Like its red brother, it thrives in hedgerows and fields. If you are out in the evening you will notice that its white flowers are all wide open. The *new* flowers in particular give out a fragrant scent at sundown and are most attractive to moths.

*   *   *

WILD ROSE

. . . and the desert shall rejoice, and blossom as the rose.

When the prophet Isaiah wrote these words thousands of years ago the rose must have been the same lovely symbol of summer that it is to-day. There are several different kinds of wild rose, but the most common is the dainty dog rose, which abounds in nearly every hedge and thicket. It is the largest of the British wild roses, and, as you probably know, grows very vigorously, with long branches protected by vicious hooks. The leaves are broken up into five or seven tooth-edged leaflets and the blooms are of a delicate shell-pink, with five petals which close gently into a little cup in the evening.

Another type of wild rose is the sweet briar, which grows on quite a small bush. The leaves are tiny and give out an unmistakably sweet smell. The flowers are also small and pink.

Sometimes you will find a rose with white flowers more closely clustered than the dog rose. This is the field rose.

*   *   *

HIP HONEY

The scarlet berries of the wild rose are called hips. They are a very valuable food and can be made into a most delicious honey. Why don't you make some yourself? Here is the way it is done, and maybe your mother will help you, if you haven't had much cooking practice.

Gather a pint of hips when they are fully ripe, after the first frost. Wash them thoroughly and cook in an enamel pan with two pints of water. Bring to the boil and simmer till the hips are soft. Mash the hips with a wooden spoon and strain through a jelly bag, allowing the juice to drip overnight. Measure the hip juice, make it up to 1½ pints with water and add apple pulp made by cooking 12 ozs. of cooking apples in a teacupful of water till soft. Bring juice and pulp to the boil, stir in 2 lb. of sugar and continue cooking till the honey sets on a cold plate.

*　　*　　*

FORGET-ME-NOT

You will recognise the little blue forget-me-not growing close to the edge of the ditch. There are several legends told about the forget-me-not and how it was given its name. Perhaps you have not heard this one.

Once, at the world's beginning, an angel was sent to deliver a message to a holy man who dwelt in a desert. On his way he saw a lovely girl sitting by a well and braiding her hair with blue forget-me-nots. The angel fell in love with her and for a while they lived happily together, until he remembered one day that he had not delivered the message with which he had been trusted. In bitter shame he flew back to Heaven to ask forgiveness, but the gates were closed against him. As he stood there weeping the Archangel Gabriel appeared and said, " You must people the earth with the Children of the Sky before you can bring a daughter of the earth to Heaven."

But the angel could not understand this, so he went back to his beautiful bride and asked her if she could find an explanation.

She took some of the lovely little forget-me-nots from her hair and said : " Yes, I think I know. These flowers which reflect the exquisite colour of Heaven must be the Children of the Sky."

So the angel and his bride wandered hand in hand over the Earth and planted forget-me-nots in every country, and when their task was finished he carried her up in his arms to the gate of Heaven.

Now we have come to a break in the hedge and a stile. On the other side a little path wanders temptingly up the side of a sloping meadow. A few brown cows are placidly chewing among the buttercups and at the top of the hill there is a wood. Let us climb the stile and see what we can find.

* * *

BUTTERCUPS AND DAISIES

> When daisies pied and violets blue
> And lady-smocks all silver-white
> And cuckoo-buds of yellow hue
> Do paint the meadows with delight. . . .

SHAKESPEARE.

You could not find a hayfield without buttercups and daisies, and both are among the commonest flowers of the countryside, but you must have them in your collection. A study of these two very ordinary flowers will help you to understand a little of the different *families* to which flowers belong.

As you begin to learn more about botany—which is the name for the study of plant life—you will soon begin to recognise these families. The names of the various families are rather difficult to remember at first because they are all in Latin, and this is so that botanists and scientists all over the world can understand each other by using the same language. The bird families also have Latin names for the same reason, and doctors use Latin for the names of medicines.

If you pull up a buttercup, you will see that the roots are what we call " bulbous." The golden flower is very lovely when you look at it closely, and has five petals of equal size and shape. Petals of equal size and shape are a characteristic of this family, of which other members are the anemone, which we shall find in the wood, and the lesser celandine, which we saw in the ditch. If you pull out a petal of a buttercup, you will see that, at its base, there is a little pocket containing honey.

Many garden flowers, such as the columbine, are related to

the buttercup, and their family is called *Ranunculaceæ*. In our gardens we treat the buttercup as a weed, because it spreads so rapidly, but a field of golden buttercups is a lovely sight. If the weather is mild, you will often see them in bloom in December.

Now look at the little daisy, the flower that grows everywhere and blooms nearly all the year round—the humble little daisy which closes up its petals tight in the evening and opens them to the sun as he rises again ! Look at it carefully and you will understand at once how differently it is made from the buttercup. Pull out one of the pink-tipped petals and you will see that the petal is a complete flower in itself, and that even the yellow centre part is made up of tiny tube-shaped flowers. It is the commonest of a very large plant family called *Compositæ*, which means compound or composite, because each " flower " consists of a cluster of flowers. Once you have understood this you will soon see how many relations the daisy has—thistles, dandelions, sunflowers, marguerites, marigolds and asters are some of them.

*　　　*　　　*

COWSLIPS

> *The cowslips tall her pensioners be ;*
> *In their gold coats spots you see ;*
> *Those be rubies, fairy favours,*
> *In those freckles live their savours.*

SHAKESPEARE.

If the field we are crossing is one which has been a hayfield for many years, you may find from April onwards that the cowslips are growing thickly. They are not a very common flower and like to be left alone, so they do not spread rapidly nor grow on land which has been ploughed up and then turned into pasture again. The leaves are rather dark, like those of the primrose, and grow close to the ground. The stalks grow six to eight inches high and bear clusters of the pale yellow fragrant blooms. Cowslips are like a collection of little primroses hanging in a cluster from one stem. Country people love cowslips and make them into a delicious wine, while the children make cowslip balls. This is quite easy to do. First pull off the flower heads and then sew them on to a thread or length of wool. Pack the heads close together as you thread them on, and when you have got on all you can, take the two ends and tie them together. Pull the ends firm as the flowers meet and spread them out and you have a soft ball of glowing yellow blossom.

* * *

SCABIOUS

From June to September in a dry part of our meadow we shall find the pale lilac flowers of the field scabious. The flower heads are carried on the end of a long, hairy stalk. The leaves are oblong and the lowest bluntly toothed. The scabious with the smaller, rounder flower heads is called the Devil's Bit scabious, and the leaves are oval and *not* toothed. There is another close relation, called the lesser scabious, but they all make a brave show with their rather unusual colour, and you should try to get at least two of them for your collection.

* * *

THE POPPY

There are several different kinds of poppy in this country, but the commonest is the scarlet poppy, which is most usually seen in the farmer's cornfields, where it is really a weed. Sometimes you can see the growing grain splashed with great scarlet stains as the poppies reach up to the sun. Not often will they be found in ordinary meadows, but they grow vigorously in waste ground and poor soil and are always much prettier growing than picked.

All poppies have only four petals. The stems are tall and branched, with bristly hairs on them. If you pick them, your hands will be stained brown with the thick white juice. If you open the big seed box with its flattish top, rather like a corrugated-iron roof, you will see that it is divided up by little walls into partitions which are packed with tiny green seeds. When the petals fall this ingenious seed box turns brown and cracks open, so that the little ripe seeds are shaken out by the wind.

Poppies are specially grown in the East for the white juice, which is dried and used as a powerful drug called opium. Remember that this is poison. Another kind of poppy, with a yellow flower, is the horned poppy, but you are not likely to see this in our meadow because it generally grows by the seashore.

*　　　*　　　*

SCARLET PIMPERNEL

Sometimes in the field, perhaps in the hedgerow and often on waste ground, will be found the little scarlet pimpernel. The dainty little flowers are like red stars which close in the evenings, and because they are never open in cool weather the country folk call the pimpernel the Poor-Man's-Weather-Glass.

*　　　*　　　*

LADY'S SMOCK

If the lower part of our field is damp or swampy, you will find the pretty pale pink or lilac lady's smock, which, you will remember, Shakespeare described as "painting the meadows with delight." The flowers have four petals and grow separately from the top of the stem. In some parts of the country they are called Milkmaids or Cuckoo flowers.

*　　　*　　　*

BIRD'S-FOOT TREFOIL

Before we go up to the wood you may have noticed, at any time between June and October, little yellow flowers tinted with red growing in clusters quite near to the ground. If you look at these carefully you will see that they belong to the pea family, because the flower has a big petal at the back, two "wings" at the side and two more petals in front. This little golden flower is called in some places Lady's Slipper, but more generally Bird's-foot Trefoil, because the flowers are followed by little seed pods which, when clustered together, look rather like a bird's claw.

There are many other flowers to be found in the pasture fields—the lovely ox-eye daisies and the different kinds of golden-starred St. John's Worts. Then there are the vetches and the little wild pansies and, of course, the red and white clovers. Down by the stream you will find the sweet-smelling, heavy, creamy heads of meadow-sweet or Queen of the Meadows. But you will have to go back another day to find these, for we must go up to the wood.

*   *   *

TO DAFFODILS

Fair daffodils, we weep to see
You haste away so soon ;
As yet the early-rising sun
Has not attain'd his noon.
    Stay, stay
Until the hasting day
    Has run
But to the evensong ;
And, having pray'd together, we
Will go with you along.

We have short time to stay, as you,
We have as short a spring ;
As quick a growth to meet decay,
As you, or anything.
    We die
As your hours do, and dry
    Away
Like to the summer's rain ;
Or as the pearls of morning's dew
Ne'er to be found again.

ROBERT HERRICK

*   *   *

When the days are still short and dark and when the sun seems to have forgotten us, then comes spring's bravest herald, the daffodil. I dare say you have grown them in bowls of fibre indoors, and I'm sure you will have welcomed them in your own garden and on the barrows in the streets without realising that a shorter, sturdier variety grows wild in open woods and pastures and that to see hundreds of them nodding and swaying their gracious heads is an unforgettable sight. The poet Wordsworth, who died nearly one hundred years ago and who lived in the Lake District, once wrote beautifully of them :

> *I wander'd lonely as a cloud*
> *That floats on high o'er vales and hills,*
> *When all at once I saw a crowd,*
> *A host, of golden daffodils ;*
> *Beside the lake, beneath the trees,*
> *Fluttering and dancing in the breeze.*

And so, in March and April, for too short a time, we shall find daffodils on the edge of our wood spreading a little way down the slope of the meadow. Pick some if you will, because " they haste away so soon," but *never, never* dig up the bulbs. Leave them to gladden another spring. I always associate daffodils with Easter and love their other name, which is Lent Lily.

* * *

WOOD ANEMONE

With the daffodils comes the dainty little wind flower, or wood anemone, which is found more often in sheltered woods and copses than in the meadows. The flowers are usually white, just tinged with pink, but sometimes they have a purplish tinge. They are of the same family as the butter-cup—*Ranunculaceæ*—and they grow in colonies, so that the copses in March are thickly carpeted with them after one or two warmer days. The flowers are unbelievably frail and dainty—one to each slender stalk—and their heads hang so that they can turn their backs to the gentlest breeze. *Anemos* is the Greek word for wind, so you can see how this flower got its name.

THE PRIMROSE

There is something very coy and prim about the primrose, for it loves the shade and hides its wan but welcome beauty under its dark, wrinkled leaves, which grow larger as the spring days lengthen. But we all love her, for she is another of spring's messengers and her pale beauty stars the slopes of the copse and the banks of the streams in the woods with the anemones. She is the chief member of a very large family called *Primulaceæ*—the garden primula and the cowslip belong to this, too.

*   *   *

THE VIOLET

Now fades the last long streak of snow,
Now burgeons every maze of quick
About the flowering squares and thick
By ashen roots the violets blow.

ALFRED TENNYSON

By now you will have noticed that many of the flowers which grow in the woods are modest and retiring; "modest" is the word generally used to describe the violet, which nestles down amongst its heart-shaped leaves clinging very close to the ground. The cultivated violets which you can buy from the flower-shop or from hawkers in the city streets are grown specially in Cornwall and the Scilly Islands, where the winter is short and warm, and although these are very lovely you can have no idea what violets should be until you have seen them growing wild on a sunny bank or in the dappled shadows of a wood.

The sweet violet—so named because of its beautiful perfume—is one of the very earliest of spring flowers and blooms from March to May. The flowers vary in colour from pure white to reddish purple or blue. The stalk is generally short, but looks even shorter because it bends over at the top. Later in the year, in May, we may find the dog violet, which has no scent and whose blooms are always purple. In the

99

olden days the violet was used for medicine as well as for its perfume.

There are several other members of the violet family, but you are not likely to find them in the woods.

* * *

BLUEBELLS

The bluebell, or wild hyacinth—and you will see at once why it is like the hyacinth that you can buy in a pot or which grows in your garden—loves the shade, and although occasionally it may be found in a meadow, it is common in copses and woods nearly everywhere. When you pick it, it looks blue, but when you see tens of thousands of them flowering in the woods in May they spread a misty purple carpet that is difficult to describe. A bluebell wood is one of Nature's most wonderful sights, for although the flowers have no marked fragrance they have a beauty all their own. The stem grows from a bulb, and is one foot or more high. The bells hang from one side of the stem, which bends gracefully, just as if its dainty burden was about to ring a fairy chime.

A lot of people go specially into the country to pick bluebells, which has always seemed rather stupid because the biggest bunch of the flowers in a jar at home makes a poor show compared with their beauty in the woods. They soon wilt in the sun, too, but it is true that their glory is very tempting, so if you feel you must take some home, nip off the juicy stems carefully *above* the ground and do not drag them up so that the white part of the stem shows. If you do this the bulbs are spoiled and will not flower next year.

* * *

FOXGLOVES

Stately and tall, the graceful foxglove grows in the open spaces of the wood. I suppose it is the tallest flower you are likely to find here, for sometimes it will grow to a height of five feet. The Latin name is *Digitalis*, which means finger, and when you examine the flowers you can see why. Some people say that once it was called *Folk's-glove*, meaning a glove for the fairies, and this also is easy to understand. The handsome, bell-shaped flowers grow in a spike and droop as they expand so that they are protected from the rain dripping from the trees. The blooms are a deep rose-pink and inside are spotted like a leopard skin. When they are growing they are lovely, but when the petals have fallen and the seeds are ripening the bare stalks are rather ugly. It is best not to pick the foxglove, for it is poisonous.

* * *

DEADLY NIGHTSHADE

Before we leave the wood I want to warn you about the deadly nightshade which you may see occasionally growing in waste places. It is, as its name suggests, a very deadly poison and should never be touched. It grows into rather an erect plant some three to four feet high, with branching stems and rather large leaves. The flowers are a dingy sort of purple and not very big or noticeable, but they turn into round, purple-black berries, rather like blackcurrants.

Another near relation which is almost as dangerous is the bittersweet. The differences are easy to remember, though, because with the bittersweet the bluish-purple flowers grow in *clusters*, while the nightshade flowers are solitary. The berries of the bittersweet are a bright scarlet, while the nightshade berries are *purple-black*.

* * *

Now I have told you just enough about our wayside and woodland flowers to start you off exploring and collecting for yourself. It is a good plan to make a collection to look at in the winter evenings when you are sitting round the fire and longing for the spring. Always pick the finest specimens you can find and, when you get home, lay each one carefully between sheets of clean blotting-paper and press them flat under a pile of books. When they are well dried you fix them in an exercise book, or something bigger, with little strips of sticky transparent paper. It is a good idea to divide your collection into the flower " families " I have told you about and, of course, you should record where and when you found each specimen. If you want to make wild flowers a hobby, you will have to read one or more of the books I recommend in the Book Section, so that you have a full guide with plenty of pictures to help you.

* * *

> *I know a bank whereon the wild thyme blows,*
> *Where oxlips and the nodding violet grows,*
> *Quite over-canopied with luscious woodbine,*
> *With sweet musk-roses and with eglantine ;*
> *There sleeps Titania some time of the night,*
> *Lull'd in these flowers with dances and delight ;*
> *And there the snake throws her enamell'd skin,*
> *Weed wide enough to wrap a fairy in.*

SHAKESPEARE

The Seasons

IT is in the countryside that we can best watch the miracle
of the changing seasons, for the birds and trees and flowers
and farmer's fields are all witnesses of the unseen power that
pushes the snowdrop through the frozen earth to greet the
spring, ripens the harvests, and sends the hedgehog to sleep
for the winter.

Poets great and humble have always sung to the seasons,
and I have chosen some examples for you to read here. The
first was written by a little girl of nine. It was the first
poem she had ever written.

THE SEASONS

When Spring comes,
All the birds build their nests.
The blackbird sings his joyous song,
The buds begin to burst,
And the lambs are at their play.

When Summer comes,
She throws about her everywhere
Leaves and grass and flowers,
And all the woods and fields
She mingles with buttercups and daisies.

And when Winter comes,
He with him brings
Driving winds and stinging sleet
And softly falling snow,
And the fog hangs thick and grey.

But of all the seasons
Autumn is the crown.
With shining fields and ripening fruit
The yellow leaves are patched with red,
And all the world is soaked with dew.

SPRING

Poets have always loved the spring.   Here are seven poems
—all rather different.

PIPPA'S SONG

The year's at the spring,
And day's at the morn ;
Morning's at seven ;
The hill-side's dew-pearled ;
The lark's on the wing ;
The snail's on the thorn :
God's in His heaven—
All's right with the world !

ROBERT BROWNING

FEBRUARY

To-day I saw the catkins blow,
Altho' the hills are white with snow ;

While throstles sang, " The sun is good,"
They waved their banners in the wood.

They come to greet the lurking Spring
As messengers from Winter's King.

And thus they wave while Winter reigns,
While his cold grip still holds the plains.

Oh, tho' the hills are white with snow,
To-day I saw the catkins blow !

DOROTHY UNA RATCLIFFE

SPRING

(There is a country saying that Spring has not come until you can set your foot on seven daisies at once.)

THE SPRING

" Oh ! how do you know
  When Spring has come ?
Still falls the snow
  And the birds are dumb."

The grass will wear
  A brighter tone,
The thrush will dare
  To carol alone.

The silver rain
  Will gently fall,
The woods will gain
  The blackbird's call.

But the way to tell,
  And the surest way,
Is to find a dell,
  Where the breezes play,

And seek and seek
  Where the daisy, soon,
Will show like a meek
  White baby moon ;

When your foot treads,
  With tender fear,
On seven white heads,—
  Then Spring is here.

DOROTHY UNA RATCLIFFE

SPRING MORNING

Now the moisty wood discloses
Wrinkled leaves of primèroses,
While the birds, they flute and sing :
Build your nests, for here is Spring.

All about the open hills
Daisies shew their peasant frills,
Washed and white and newly spun
For a festival of sun.

Like a blossom from the sky,
Drops a yellow butterfly,
Dancing down the hedges grey
Snow-bestrewn till yesterday.

Squirrels skipping up the trees
Smell how Spring is in the breeze,
While the birds, they flute and sing :
Build your nests, for here is Spring.

FRANCES CORNFORD

Spring, the sweet Spring, is the year's pleasant king ;
Then blooms each thing, then maids dance in a ring,
Cold doth not sting, the pretty birds do sing—
Cuckoo, jug-jug, pu-we, to-witta-woo !

The palm and may make country houses gay,
Lambs frisk and play, the shepherds pipe all day,
And we hear ay birds tune this merry lay,
Cuckoo, jug-jug, pu-we, to-witta-woo !

SPRING

The fields breathe sweet, the daisies kiss our feet,
Young lovers meet, old wives a-sunning sit,
In every street these tunes our ears do greet—
Cuckoo, jug-jug, pu-we, to-witta-woo !
Spring, the sweet Spring !

THOMAS NASHE

HOME THOUGHTS, FROM ABROAD

Oh, to be in England
Now that April's there,
And whoever wakes in England
Sees, some morning, unaware,
That the lowest boughs and the brushwood sheaf
Round the elm-tree bole are in tiny leaf,
While the chaffinch sings on the orchard bough
In England—now !

And after April, when May follows,
And the whitethroat builds, and all the swallows !
Hark, where my blossom'd pear-tree in the hedge
Leans to the field and scatters on the clover
Blossoms and dewdrops—at the bent spray's edge—
That's the wise thrush ; he sings each song twice over,
Lest you should think he never could recapture
The first fine careless rapture !
And though the fields look rough with hoary dew,
All will be gay when noontide wakes anew
The buttercups, the little children's dower
—Far brighter than this gaudy melon-flower.

ROBERT BROWNING

WINTER HAS DEPARTED

There are green leaves on the trees ;
  The winter has fled and the noon
Of spring is over the leas—
  The earth will be colourful soon.

The light on the shore is gold
  Where the drifting sands have been blown,
For winter's knell has been tolled,
  And the earth delivers her own.

There is a song on the downs,
  And warm is the breath of the wind,
The streets are bright in the towns,
  For winter has fallen behind.

The sun rides high in the sky,
  And the lambs are free of the fold,
And new-winged birds can all fly,
  Their chant is the chant of the bold.

And the heart of man beats fast,
  His voice with a new song shall ring,
The pangs of birth are the last,
  For now is the high noon of Spring.

CLARENCE WINCHESTER

*　　*　　*

And here is a prose passage about the spring in a wood.   I think it is an unforgettable description.

GROVELY WOOD IN MARCH

We rode up through Grovely Wood.   At every season of the year this wood is beautiful, but just now it is very lovely indeed. Spring's sudden visit seemed to have caught even the trees unawares, and they are hurrying to catch up with her, or, to put it in another way, Spring is positively bustling them into their clothes. As we rode I noticed that fresh colour was showing everywhere against the sombre black of their winter nakedness. Green predominated, but the beeches were covered with a pinkish film ; here and there a drift of almond-coloured palm showed against a background of dark-green spruce ; while around us on every side green honeysuckle twined eagerly amongst the breaking hazel buds.

But the loveliest thing of all was the continuous chorus of the birds. When we entered the wood a pigeon or two clattered noisily away, a blackbird rattled his danger signal, and a jay screamed a hoarse warning of our intrusion. But when we arrived in the middle of the wood we stopped for a few moments to listen, and all around us was song in praise of Spring, sung by an invisible choir—coos, chuckles, chirrupings, baritone from the blackbird, contralto from the thrush, and every now and again a thin treble thread of melody from the smaller songbirds.

A. G. STREET

*   *   *

SUMMER

I have always liked Robert Louis Stevenson's description of the sun as "the gardener of the world." It was Stevenson who wrote *Treasure Island*.

SUMMER SUN

Great is the sun, and wide he goes
Through empty heaven without repose ;
And in the blue and glowing days
More thick than rain he showers his rays.

Though closer still the blinds we pull
To keep the shady parlour cool,
Yet he will find a chink or two
To slip his golden fingers through.

The dusty attic, spider-clad,
He, through the keyhole, maketh glad ;
And through the broken edge of tiles,
Into the laddered hayloft smiles.

Meantime his golden face around
He bares to all the garden ground,
And sheds a warm and glittering look
Among the ivy's inmost nook.

Above the hills, along the blue,
Round the bright air with footing true,
To please the child, to paint the rose,
The gardener of the World, he goes.

ROBERT LOUIS STEVENSON

*　　　*　　　*

AUTUMN

Here is one of the greatest poems ever written to autumn. You may find some of it a little difficult to understand at first, but after you have read it—or better still, had it read to you—several times you will realise how lovely it is.

ODE TO AUTUMN

Season of mists and mellow fruitfulness !
Close bosom-friend of the maturing sun ;
Conspiring with him how to load and bless
With fruit the vines that round the thatch-eaves run ;
To bend with apples the moss'd cottage-trees,
And fill all fruit with ripeness to the core ;
To swell the gourd, and plump the hazel shells
With a sweet kernel ; to set budding more
And still more, later flowers for the bees,
Until they think warm days will never cease,
For Summer has o'er-brimm'd their clammy cells.

Who hath not seen thee oft amid thy store?
Sometimes whoever seeks abroad may find
Thee sitting careless on a granary floor,
Thy hair soft-lifted by the winnowing wind;
Or on a half-reap'd furrow sound asleep,
Drowsed with the fumes of poppies, while thy hook
Spares the next swath and all its twinèd flowers;
And sometimes like a gleaner thou dost keep
Steady thy laden head across a brook;
Or by a cider-press, with patient look,
Thou watchest the last oozings, hours by hours.

Where are the songs of Spring?   Ay, where are they?
Think not of them, thou hast thy music too—
While barrèd clouds bloom the soft-dying day,
And touch the stubble-plains with rosy hue;
Then in a wailful choir the small gnats mourn
Among the river-sallows, borne aloft
Or sinking as the light wind lives or dies;
And full-grown lambs loud bleat from hilly bourn;
Hedge-crickets sing; and now with treble soft
The redbreast whistles from a garden-croft,
And gathering swallows twitter in the skies.

JOHN KEATS

*　　*　　*

Here is something very different. It was written one
autumn evening in wartime, and although it was not really
intended for children, I believe you will understand it. The
South-west wind is the wind that blows most often on Great
Britain, and is called the prevailing wind.

THE FIRST STORM OF AUTUMN

In the evening he came stealing out of the west. Gently at
first—a few warm puffs from the Atlantic moving the tree tops
but barely shaking from them the turning leaves. England's own
wind. The wind that reaches us first and comes untainted from

the sea to cross our coloured counties to tell us that summer has gone again and that the year is dying.

He always comes this way. Often he is here before we are aware of him—whirling the dust in the gutters and chasing the clouds out of the western horizon.

Yesterday he came just as dusk was falling. First he stirred the head of the great Scots pine at the edge of the Common, and then rustled the vivid, scarlet leaves of the creeper hiding the ugliness of manbuilt walls. He fanned the glow of a bonfire into an orange flame and flung up a plume of sweet-smelling smoke and trailed it as incense in his wake. He brought with him, too, the savour of the fresh, ploughed fields across the lane.

Then he sighed and was gone. And we shut out the night while the groping searchlights silently stabbed the sky with mechanical beauty.

At midnight he returned. Stronger now and purposeful. He snatched at the loose briar outside the window and tossed it petulantly against the pane. He sang through the tree tops, and whistled through the house, bringing triumphantly the first storm of autumn. He flung the still warm rain across the sleeping shires while, under the eaves, the gutters whispered, sang, and then were dumb as they choked with fallen leaves. The moon came up with hidden face and with no chance to show her beauty as the wind piled up a screen of scudding clouds, tore them apart, and then tossed them contemptuously over the eastern plains towards the wilderness of the North Sea. He howled in the chimney and brought the still ungathered apples in the orchard thudding down to the sodden grass.

As the night waned and the storm-tossed eastern sky lightened with the dawn he gathered his strength triumphantly and roared and blustered in his might. Far out in the ocean he whipped the grey waves to white-capped fury. He nearly smothered a convoy homeward bound, and gave a helping hand to a flying boat of Coastal Command winging eastward from patrol. He tore down the Channel and made of Biscay an inferno. He blotted out the mountains of Wales with flying rain, howled round Stonehenge and brought down the rotting wood in the forests of the South. He swept across the dingy cities of the Midlands, to meet the

*dirty tide coming up London river.   He plucked at loose slates
and tiles and brought down tottering chimney pots.   He greeted
sleepy firewatchers in the towns and tore at the hair of a green-
jerseyed land girl at the gate of a Hertfordshire field.*

*Then he washed the sky clean.   The grey clouds vanished and
the sun came out.   Great galleons of fluffy white sailed majestic-
ally across the blue.   On the lawns, in the gardens, across the
fields and in the streets lay the wreckage of his fury—twigs, dead
leaves and useless rubbish.*

*Higher climbed the sun over Britain and we saw the miracle
of autumn in a single night—the boughs of the chestnut stripped,
the oak leaves a richer gold and, out on the Common, the bracken
turned to russet.*

*The wind that is forever England had come and gone again,
as he will always do.*

D. J. DESMOND

*   *   *

WINTER

*Sweet blackbird is silenced with chaffinch and thrush,
Only waistcoated robin still chirps in the bush :
Soft sun-loving swallows have mustered in force,
And winged in the spice-teeming southlands their course.*

*Plump housekeeper dormouse has tucked himself neat,
Just a brown ball in moss with a morsel to eat :
Armed hedgehog has huddled him into the hedge,
While frogs scarce miss freezing deep down in the sedge.*

Soft swallows have left us alone in the lurch,
But robin sits whistling to us from his perch :
If I were red robin, I'd pipe you a tune,
Would make you despise all the beauties of June.

But, since that cannot be, let us draw round the fire,
Munch chestnuts, tell stories, and stir the blaze higher :
We'll comfort pinched robin with crumbs, little man,
Till he'll sing us the very best song that he can.

CHRISTINA ROSSETTI

WINTER

When icicles hang by the wall
And Dick the shepherd blows his nail,
And Tom bears logs into the hall,
And milk comes frozen home in pail ;
When blood is nipt, and ways be foul,
Then nightly sings the staring owl
          Tuwhoo !
Tuwhit ! tuwhoo ! A merry note !
While greasy Joan doth keel the pot.

When all aloud the wind doth blow,
And coughing drowns the parson's saw,
And birds sit brooding in the snow,
And Marian's nose looks red and raw ;
When roasted crabs hiss in the bowl—
Then nightly sings the staring owl
          Tuwhoo !
Tuwhit ! tuwhoo ! A merry note !
While greasy Joan doth keel the pot.

WILLIAM SHAKESPEARE

Here are three beautiful little verses describing the seasons. They are easy to learn and to remember.

THE YEAR

The crocus, while the days are dark,
Unfolds its saffron sheen ;
At April's touch, the crudest bark
Discovers gems of green.

Then sleep the seasons, full of might ;
While slowly swells the pod
And rounds the peach, and in the night
The mushroom bursts the sod.

The winter falls ; the frozen rut
Is bound with silver bars,
The snowdrift heaps against the hut
And night is pierced with stars.

COVENTRY PATMORE

* * *

WEATHER SIGNS

Everyone talks and worries about the weather. In England we are lucky really, because it is always changing, and although sometimes it is a nuisance to take a raincoat whenever we want to go for a walk, it is more fun to have a varied climate than to live in a country where you know that rain is going to come for certain at the same time each year, and when it will be hot and when it will be cold. The incomparable beauty of our land is largely due to the weather, and in the country all the farmer's work depends upon it. And so, through the years, country people have passed down from father to son all sorts of quaint prophecies and sayings about the weather, and some of them you will find most reliable. You can soon learn to read weather signs for yourself, and, of course, the clouds are the best guide if you want to become a weather prophet. Here are some suggestions to help you.

First you must remember the four main types of cloud formation, which have Latin names easy enough to remember when you have learned what the names mean.

First, the *Cirrus* or thread cloud. Cirrus really means curl of hair, but you will recognise these clouds because they are wispy, straight streaks sometimes called " Mare's Tails." They forecast wind.

Next, the *Cumulus* or heap cloud. (Cumulus is the Latin for heap.) This is sometimes called the " Woolpack," because it is like a great, fluffy pile of cotton-wool. These clouds do not usually mean rain.

Then the *Stratus* or flat cloud. Stratus means a bed covering, so this is easy enough to recognise. They are generally seen high up in the evening across the sunset sky in level bars. Sometimes on a dull day the stratus clouds lie very low, rather in the form of fog.

The rain cloud is the *Nimbus*—a dense layer of dark, shapeless cloud with ragged edges. When you see this cloud effect you can be certain that rain is on the way. There are different variations of the Nimbus, such as the dark-edged *Cumulo-Nimbus* thunder clouds, and you will soon learn to recognise them. Nimbus, by the way, comes from the Latin word for the cloud which surrounded the ancient gods when they appeared on earth.

*　　*　　*

THE CLOUD

I bring fresh showers for the thirsting flowers
  From the seas and the streams ;
I bear light shade for the leaves when laid
  In their noonday dreams.
From my wings are shaken the dews that waken
  The sweet buds every one,
When rocked to rest on their Mother's breast,
  As she dances about the sun.
I wield the flail of the lashing hail,
  And whiten the green plains under ;
And then again I dissolve it in rain,
  And laugh as I pass in thunder.

PERCY BYSSHE SHELLEY

*　　*　　*

When studying the weather you will remember, of course, that the direction of the wind will help you to forecast what weather is on the way. You know that wind from the west or south-west is likely to bring rain and unsettled weather. An east wind is colder, but in summer it generally brings fine days. In winter the east wind is the prophet of frost and snow storms. The north-easter is the coldest wind we know.

*　　*　　*

Here are some old " weather sayings."

" *If the Ash comes out before the Oak,*
  The Summer will be a regular soak ;
  If the Oak comes out before the Ash,
  Then the Summer will be a splash."

" *Saint Swithin's Day if thou be fair,*
  'Twill rain for forty days no mair.
  Saint Swithin's Day if thou dost rain,
  For forty days it will remain."

(St. Swithin's Day is July 15.)

117

" If the North wind blows on Michaelmas Day
The month of October is sunny and gay."

(Michaelmas Day—the Church Feast day of St. Michael
and All Angels—is September 29.)

" A cold April the barn will fill."

" Button to chin
Till May be in.
Ne'er cast a clout,
Till May is out ! "

* * *

On a summer night, if the stars seem brighter than usual,
then wind and rain are on the way. In winter, when the wind
is in the north or east and the stars blaze and twinkle, then
the weather will turn colder and the earth will be gripped
with great frosts.

* * *

When the moon shines clear without a misty rim it will be
fine weather. When she is compassed round with a halo,
wind or rain follows soon.

When the sun arises red and fiery, wind and rain are on
the way. If at sun rising it is cloudy and the clouds vanish
as the sun rises, it will be a fine day.

A red sunset foretells fine weather, unless it is muddy and
misty, when rain will follow.

* * *

THE WIND IN A FROLIC

The wind one morning sprang up from sleep,
Saying, " Now for a frolic ! now for a leap !
Now for a mad-cap galloping chase !
I'll make a commotion in every place ! "
So it swept with a bustle right through the town,
Cracking the signs and scattering down
Shutters ; and whisking, with merciless squalls,
Old women's bonnets and gingerbread stalls.
There never was heard a much lustier shout,
As the apples and oranges trundled about ;
And the urchins that stand with their thievish eyes
For ever on watch, ran off each with a prize.

Then away to the fields it went, blustering and humming,
All the cattle all wondered whatever was coming ;
It plucked by the tails the grave matronly cows,
And tossed the colts' manes all over their brows ;
Till offended at such an unusual salute,
They all turned their backs, and stood sulky and mute.

Then it rushed like a monster on cottage and farm,
Striking their dwellers with sudden alarm ;
And they ran out like bees in a midsummer swarm ;—
There were dames with their kerchiefs tied over their caps,
To see if their poultry were free from mishaps;
The turkeys they gobbled, the geese screamed aloud ;
The hens crept to roost in a terrified crowd ;
There was rearing of ladders, and logs laying on,
Where the thatch from the roof threatened soon to be gone.

But the wind had swept on, and had met in a lane
With a schoolboy, who panted and struggled in vain ;
For it tossed him and twirled him, then passed and he stood
With his hat in a pool and his shoes in the mud.

COUNTRY SCRAP-BOOK

Then away went the wind in its holiday glee,
And now it was far on the billowy sea,
And the lordly ships felt its staggering blow,
And the little boats darted to and fro.
But lo ! it was night, and it sank to rest
On the sea-bird's rock in the gleaming west,
Laughing to think, in its fearful fun,
How little of mischief it really had done.

WILLIAM HOWITT

Here are two verses of a very lovely poem by William Blake called *Night*. They seem to be a particularly suitable way of saying " good-bye " to the seasons.

The sun descending in the west,
The evening star does shine ;
The birds are silent in their nest.
And I must seek for mine.
The moon, like a flower
In heaven's high bower,
With silent delight
Sits and smiles on the night.

Farewell, green fields and happy grove,
Where flocks have took delight :
Where lambs have nibbled, silent move
The feet of angels bright ;
Unseen they pour blessing
And joy without ceasing
On each bud and blossom,
On each sleeping bosom.

WILLIAM BLAKE

Rivers, Ponds and Streams

Dark brown is the river,
*   Golden is the sand.*
It flows along for ever,
*   With trees on either hand.*

Green leaves a-floating,
*   Castles of the foam,*
Boats of mine a-boating—
*   Where will all come home ?*

On goes the river
*   And out past the mill,*
Away down the valley,
*   Away down the hill.*

Away down the river,
*   A hundred miles or more,*
Other little children
*   Shall bring my boats ashore.*

ROBERT LOUIS STEVENSON

You cannot walk many miles in these islands without finding water. Foreigners are always amazed at the " greenness " of England and it is true that the rains which fall on our western coasts in particular keep our valleys fresh and our pastures green and in some counties, such as Devonshire, almost every lane tinkles with running water and nearly every hillside has its spring.

Our biggest rivers are but streams to our friends from the American continent or to those who have seen the Rhine,

Rhone or Danube or the mighty rivers of Russia, but, like everything else British, our rivers and streams are like no others. Whether they splash noisily down the mountain sides, or whether they flow gently and serenely to the sea, they are our own and we love them all. Many of our rivers can be explored almost from source to mouth in a small boat ; and think what a thrilling tramping holiday you could have on the banks of almost any of them. Try the turbulent Dart, for instance, with its twin sources on grim Dartmoor running through wonderful country to Totnes where it becomes tidal and runs to the sea. Or Taw and Torridge of north Devon or the incomparably beautiful Wye which is the fisherman's paradise. Then there is the majestic Severn which carries much brown water from the Midlands and the Welsh Marches to the Bristol Channel. The roaring torrents of the Lake District are unique and so are the little rills of the Shropshire highlands. The Thames valley, though much built over, is still beautiful and the little Wey is a lovely tributary. Then there are the Ouses and the Trent of the Midlands and the five Yorkshire rivers that run into the Humber. All have their own charms and all will have something special to offer you.

Water always invites me to follow. I never see a stream without wanting to climb to its source. I never find a spring without wanting to follow it to the sea, and the next time your exploring brings you to the banks of a brook you too may see with Tennyson " *the netted sunbeams dance against the sandy shallows.*"

Do you remember how dear old Ratty in Kenneth Grahame's *The Wind in the Willows* told his friend Mole there was nothing " half so much worth doing as messing about in boats " ? Whether or not you are fond of boats or keen on walking I do think Ratty was right. Water should be messed about with ! No need to hurry by a river. Stroll by it, sit by it, dip your toes into it, swim in it, float on it and above all things watch what is going on round you.

Let us look first for some of the things you may see on or around the water rather than in it.

THE MOORHEN

This is probably the commonest of all our water birds and a dainty little lady she is. You will find her on ponds, lakes and rivers that are edged with reeds and rushes and will recognise her by the white under her black tail and red bands round her legs. When she is in the water you will know her by her scarlet bill, which is yellow at the tip. Moorfowl nest amongst the rushes beside the water, but have been known to build in a low bush or tree. In summer when father and mother take their family of chicks for an evening paddle in and out of the rushes they are particularly entertaining. They can dive and swim under water.

*   *   *

THE KINGFISHER

" The secret splendour of the brook."

TENNYSON

And so he is ! Most gorgeously and royally coloured of all our birds and so fast on the wing and so shy of habit that he can be seen only if you are very still and very patient. Let me try to describe him. A small bird not more than eight inches in length. His chief colour is blue—a dazzling royal blue with a suggestion of rich green on the top of the head and wings. In the sunshine as he flashes past it sometimes looks as if his under parts are gilded, but when he is still you will see they are a rich chestnut. There is some white on the throat and ears. His bill is long and sharp, and has to be, for he lives mostly on little fish which he spears from the water. He kills the fish by beating it against a branch or a stone and then swallows it head first. Oddly enough he cannot digest fish bones and brings them up again rather in the same way as the owl disgorges pellets of fur which he has swallowed.

The kingfisher nests at the end of a tunnel about three feet long in the river bank and the nest is made of the dry fish bones which it cannot digest ! Rather in the same way as the robin takes over a kingdom in the garden and fights all rivals who cross its boundaries, so does the kingfisher seem to keep to one stretch of the river as a hunting-ground. Although he is difficult to see at first you can be certain that if you wait long and quietly enough he will come back to fish in the same stretch, for he usually has his favourite perch overlooking the water.

* * *

SWANS

The graceful swans most usually seen on our lakes and rivers are not really wild birds at all, although two truly wild varieties do sometimes fly to Scottish lochs near the sea in the winter. The swan we know is called the mute swan and is easily recognised by its deep orange bill with a black knob at its base. I expect you know that the father swan takes a share at sitting on the eggs in the spring and that both parents are fierce and courageous and will attack anyone coming too near their nest. The babies, called cygnets, are grey when hatched and are often carried on the parent's back when they first leave the nest.

* * *

THE HERON

The heron is the biggest of our commoner birds and, I should think, the most patient. Herons nest together in a colony called a heronry, so it is not very difficult to find their haunts ; but it is not so easy to find a single heron when he is waiting for his meal. He feeds on fish, frogs, eels, insects and sometimes small water voles ; to catch them he stands motionless among the reeds and he is very, very difficult to see because he is so still. He has long, thin legs and sometimes stands on one of them and sometimes on both. His neck is long too and when fishing he seems to sink his narrow head into his shoulders with boredom ! And so he stands waiting for his meal to come to him. He never waits in vain, for sooner or later his cruel, long bill stabs the water and then the fish is swallowed head first.

The heron is most easily recognised in flight, for no other

British bird uses quite the same slow, steady beat of his wings. He can fly fast and far.

Like the rooks the herons come back to their untidy nests year after year.

*   *   *

THE WATER VOLE

Sometimes when you are standing still by the river's edge waiting for the kingfisher or the heron you may hear a sharp " plop " in the water, but however quick you are you will see nothing on the surface but the widening rings spreading towards the bank. Look carefully *under* the water and you may just see a little brown body swimming like a fish towards the under-water entrance to his home. This is the water vole, often miscalled a rat.

He is a harmless little animal except for the damage he sometimes does to the banks of streams with his burrowings. You are more likely to see him in the evenings, for he does not come out of his burrow very much in the daytime. He has long, thick, glossy reddish fur which is yellowish underneath. His sight is not good, but he can hear extremely well with his little round ears. The voles have interesting habits. The female builds a circular nest of reeds and grasses for her babies and sometimes she puts this on a floating platform in the rushes. At other times the nest is built at the end of the burrow.

Like the squirrel the little vole lays in a big store of food for the winter.

*   *   *

Of what you can see *in* the water many books have been written and if, up to now, you have never taken much interest in fish I hope you will in the future, because their study can be as interesting as that of birds and butterflies. You know, of course, that fish are that part of the animal world which passes the whole of its life in fresh or salt water and breathes by means of gills. Gills enable the fish to obtain oxygen, which is necessary to life, from air dissolved in water. Taken from water fish soon die.

I want to tell you here of the astonishing life-stories of just a few of the freshwater fish, any of which you can see for yourself if you are sufficiently interested and patient.

*   *   *

THE STICKLEBACK

The stickleback or " tiddler " is one of the commonest and smallest of any of the fish we shall find in pond, lake or stream, yet the story of his existence is as exciting and dramatic as anything Nature has to tell us.   When full grown the male never exceeds four inches in length and you will know him by the three sharp, curved spines on his back in front of the back fin.   His armament is more formidable than this, however, for he has three more spines just behind his head, two more in the middle of his belly and another in front of his lower fin.

Here then is a tiny fish equipped by Nature to be a great fighter, and indeed during the breeding season he is both fierce and fearless and no fish for his size is such a pugnacious fighter. But the odd fact is that although he is so brave a warrior he is a remarkable father and does everything for his children except lay the eggs !

But let us get on with his story.   Early in the spring male and female are much alike in their rather dull, greenish colouring, but in March or April the male is transformed into a Fairy Prince of a fish.   The dull green of his back changes into stripes, his under parts become scarlet and his sides gleam as if he was wearing burnished armour.

This is the time to look in the water for sticklebacks, for you cannot possibly mistake this pugnacious warrior for anything else.   Now he changes his habits with a vengeance, for with his " armour " he becomes quarrelsome and restless and like some of the birds we have watched together he chooses a spot of his own in the water and immediately challenges any other male that comes near, and there are many fights before the claims of the strongest are established.

Once the bounds of his kindgom are set our stickleback sets about building a nest.   Now, it is unusual for any fish to build a nest and even more unusual for a male to build a nursery without help from his mate, but the stickleback works with such a will that a tiny nest about one inch across is sometimes finished within twelve hours. First, the stickleback makes a hollow in the sandy bed of the water. In this hollow he lays minute pieces of vegetable matter as a foundation and joins them together with a sticky fluid from his own body. Next he builds up " walls " until the nest looks rather like a miniature barrel lying on its side with one end open.

His next duty is to find females who can fill his nest with eggs, but as all the other males in the same part of the stream are also in search of wives the fights now between the males are nearly always to the death. The warriors can raise and lower their spines at will and now they dash furiously at each other and fight with jaws as well in their efforts to tear each other to pieces. Sometimes an opponent gives in before he is killed, and then, as he swims sadly away, his gay colours fade to drab and he hides his shame in the shelter of the weeds. The victor flaunts himself before the females, selects a mate and guides her back to his nest. Sometimes he has to spend a long time persuading her to enter the little barrel, but at last she does so and there lays a few tiny eggs before pushing her way out of the nest at the other end. The male lets her go, for he is no longer interested in her, and inspects her eggs and repairs the nest. Then he goes forth again to find another female and yet another, until he is satisfied that the nursery is well stocked with eggs. When he has enough he stays on guard outside, gently fanning water over the eggs with his fins until they hatch. Even now he still stays on to guard the babies and keep them in the shelter of the nest until they are old enough to fend for themselves, and then it is no wonder that father stickleback seems to get old and tired very quickly and that his gay colours fade !

* * *

MINNOWS

Another little fish likely to be found in the shallows of a stream or in a pond is the minnow, but he is not such an exciting find as the stickleback. Minnows swim about in quite large shoals and that is when you are most likely to see them. They are pretty little fish between three and four inches long, generally brown above and silver below, although the males are more gaily coloured in the spring. Once the eggs are laid on the stream bottom neither father nor mother has any further interest in them and they are left to hatch out by themselves. Minnows were once considered a delicacy and the famous old angler Izaak Walton gave a recipe for a dish he called Minnow-Tansy. Perhaps you would like to try it ? The fish are gutted, but not washed, and fried with the yolk of eggs, cowslips, primrose and tansy !

*   *   *

EELS

For many centuries the life-story of the common eel has been a mystery because neither eel spawn nor " baby eels " were ever found in the inland waters of Europe. Now we know a little more and the story of an eel's journeys is as great a wonder as the migration of birds or butterflies. You know, of course, what an eel looks like—a fish with a long, snake-like body and tiny head. " As slippery as an eel " describes this strange fish very well. It seems that they are long-lived and certainly some grow up to five feet in length and to a very considerable weight.

In the spring you may see young eels swimming up our rivers from the sea, but you are more likely to find old ones in the mud at the bottom of a pond. For long it was a mystery how a big eel found its way to a pond which was not fed by a stream ; but the truth is that eels at certain times of their lives travel long distances overland. They are able to do this and to live for some time in the air because over the eel's gills are two little pouches full of water so that it is able to breathe by its gills.

So far as we know there comes a time in the life of an eel—and it may well be not until it is at least six years old—when it is seized with the same uncontrollable urge as the swallow in the autumn. Early one morning when the grass is still wet with dew the eel raises itself from its soft muddy bed and climbs out of the pond and starts its long journey. It may travel many miles overland until it finds *running* water. Down the little streams and brooks they hurry, down the broad rivers they swim, always towards the sea. And in the estuaries of the river's mouth they wait while their colouring changes to silver and even the structure of their bodies change. These changes make the eels fit for their new life in the depths of the sea and eventually they swim away into mid-Atlantic, where in the great depths of the ocean they spawn and die.

From the eggs are hatched transparent babies which are not like eels at all ; these take three years in the Atlantic to develop into baby eels which are called elvers. Every spring hundreds of thousands of these elvers—they are still nearly transparent and only about three inches long—come from the ocean and swim up our rivers and streams. And as they enter fresh water so does their colouring change and they quickly grow into the eels we know—the strange fish that is born in the depths of the sea, but which you may find full grown in the mud at the bottom of a pond hundreds of miles away. But of one thing you may be certain—if our eel lives it will find its way back to the ocean to spawn and die.

*   *   *

THE TROUT

All the different members of the trout family are beautiful and this fish is perhaps the favourite and best known of all freshwater fish. It is beautiful to look at—and although its colouring varies according to the water in which it is found it is always *spotted*—and it is a swift and daring swimmer. The trout of a forest stream will be of darker green than his brother in moorland waters, while in rocky, swift-flowing rivers he is often golden. His spots and speckles make him particularly difficult to see against the river bottom and although in almost any shallow mountain stream he will not weigh more than five or six ounces, in a big lake where there is plenty of food for him he may grow enormous and weigh up to thirty or forty pounds.

Country children catch trout with their bare hands. It's not so easy as it looks, but " tickling trout " is great fun. Try it for yourself in a shallow, swift-running stream, remembering that trout like to lie under the bank or under a large rock or stone. Roll up your sleeves, lie on the bank and, keeping very still, slip your right hand into the water *below* where you think the fish is hiding, *keeping the fingers moving gently in the water all the time*. Bring the moving fingers nearer and nearer to the trout till you can feel the fingers working up from underneath and round the fish's body. Keep the finger tips moving all the time, then close them quickly round the trout and whip it from the water.

It sounds too easy to be possible, but it *is* possible if you keep your fingers moving gently all the time and don't grab at the fish. Try it for yourself !

* * *

SALMON

I expect you know the salmon by sight even if you have only seen it on a fishmonger's slab ! The salmon is the king of British fish and it is found in many parts of the world. Much of its life is spent in the sea although it is born in the gravel of a river-bed near to the river's source. When the baby fish is hatched it sinks to the bottom of the stream and in these waters it may live for as long as two years and grow no longer than six inches. At this stage of its life it is called a parr and you will recognise it by dark bands of blue on its silvery back.

When these marks disappear our young salmon is known as a smolt and about this time comes the urge to visit the sea. Here the smolt develops a tremendous appetite and grows very quickly. If he returns from the sea within a year he is next called a grilse, though sometimes he may stay two years at sea growing bigger and stronger. Eventually, however, comes the urge to spawn and so he starts the long journey back to the river in which he was born and the instinct to reach the spawning beds in the upper reaches is so strong that only death defeats him.

The grilse coming home to spawn never turns back. At weirs or other obstacles he will leap right out of the water again and again until he either wins through or dies of exhaustion. Arriving at last in the shallows the female, with her shoulders and fins, makes a trough called a redd in the sandy bed of the stream. In this redd she lays her eggs and the male comes alongside and fertilises them by ejecting into the water a quantity of milt. The female then covers the eggs with gravel and the mounds of these redds may be seen stretching under water for many feet.

After the spawning the parent fish look very woebegone and thin, but they make for the sea again and sometimes survive to make the journey again the following year.

* * *

THE PIKE

The pike is a ferocious bully. Sometimes he is called the water-wolf or freshwater shark, and both nicknames suit him very well for he is savage and ruthless.

He is not so often found in rivers as in lakes and weedy, sluggish streams where he rules alone. You won't see him swimming in the depths very often, because he prefers to stay quite motionless under the bank or in the reeds waiting for a victim. Like all bullies he has a big appetite and will catch water-fowl or even voles in his enormous jaws.

I have read of cases where a pike has caught and devoured a salmon as big as itself, although it took some days for it to complete its meal! Specimens over fifty pounds in weight have been caught in our waters, but I do not think you will often see one. In the winter months keen fishermen try for pike with a live bait and you can imagine what a battle there is when one is hooked.

* * *

OTHER FRESHWATER FISH

I have told you a little about some of the fish with unusual habits and now have little room left to tell you of the more ordinary fish. In ponds and lakes and slow-running muddy waters lives the heavy-looking tench with a blunt head and almost square tail. The carp likes similar haunts, but he can be found nearly everywhere. He is a good-looking fellow and you will know him by two small growths that hang from the corners of his mouth. The carp grows big, lives for a long time and will eat nearly anything. It is said that in olden times the monks stocked their fish pools with carp.

The perch is another handsome fish and is sometimes called the " dandy of the stream." He is a lovely striped green with glowing red fins, but he is, sad to relate, a cannibal and makes many a meal off his young relatives. If you become interested in fishing you will want to learn about roach and dace too, but I think I have told you enough to interest you in the wild life which abounds in our rivers and streams.

* * *

THE OTTER

Before we leave the running water to explore a pond more thoroughly I must tell you something of that brave and fascinating animal that lives in and round our rivers and the sea.

You will not often see an otter because he does his hunting by night and hides by day. Although not often seen he is fairly common and lives all round our coasts and along most of our rivers and streams and by many of our bigger lakes. But a sight of him is worth a lot of patience because his habits are so engaging and interesting, and he is so brave and sagacious that few animals are more worth watching.

No better story of his life has ever been written, perhaps, than *Tarka the Otter* by H. M. Williamson, and I hope you will read this as soon as you can. I expect you know that many people get a great deal of excitement and pleasure from hunting the otter with packs of hounds. Whether or not this can be justified I do not know, but the otter does little harm and although some angry fishermen say he catches the best salmon and trout—and there seems to be no real reason why he should not—it is generally accepted that he lives on frogs and eels more than anything else.

The otter is a member of the weasel family and is rather like a large weasel to look at. The body is long—up to four feet in a full-grown dog otter—with heavy, dark brown fur above turning to yellowish grey underneath. His coat is very thick to withstand the water and his head, with short ears, is like that of a cat. His legs are short and very strong, his feet webbed, and he carries a strong tail very broad and thick at the base but tapering to a point.

The otter is a most graceful runner and swimmer. When running on land—and he runs many miles at night when hunting—he arches his strong back so that his front and hind legs are together and then springs out until his back is flat. He dives from the river bank with scarcely a splash and can swim for a long time under water, but is betrayed by a " chain " of small bubbles which burst on the surface. He is a strong swimmer, though not particularly fast—he can swim no faster than the dogs which sometimes pursue him—and it is rather puzzling to know how he can catch salmon and trout unless he drives them into the shallows first.

His home—often behind the roots of a waterside tree—is called a holt. The bitch otter is a most attentive mother and the cubs are fascinating. Like all members of the weasel family otters are extremely playful, and those who have been lucky enough to see a family at play on a moonlit night say that it is a sight to remember always. Sometimes they make slides down the river bank and others have told how they have seen otters and cubs playing hide-and-seek in a hayfield.

I hope you will be lucky and see an otter.

*　　　*　　　*

POND LIFE

We have met some of the inhabitants of the pond already, but I think you should know a little more about frogs, toads and newts. It is in the spring that you will find the frothy masses of frog-spawn in almost any pond. I expect you know how the little black tadpole with his long tail comes from the egg and how in the course of time he grows legs and loses his gills. The mystery of the tadpole's transformation is more wonderful when we consider how he has changed from fish into an air-breathing land animal. When the frog has grown he lives on insects, worms and slugs and is furnished with a very remarkable tongue which is used for catching the former. A frog can live for as long as two months at the bottom of a pond, but will die if his skin is kept away from moisture and that is why you will not often see him hopping about in the sunshine. He prefers the shade and the damp.

Did you know that a frog changes its colouring to suit his surroundings ? You can prove this by moving one from the grass of the ditch to the mould of the garden. Soon he will turn quite dark and be nearly invisible. This is the only protection the frog has against his many enemies.

Some people mistake toads for frogs, but it is not difficult to tell the difference if you look carefully. The frog jumps with long graceful hops, but the toad can only waddle. In shape the latter is shorter and thicker and his back is covered with " warts " and much drier. He is not so keen a swimmer, although he can change colour as the frog does and he has a weapon which his more nimble relation lacks. At the side of his head are two glands which contain a milky fluid. When the toad is frightened these glands give off this fluid which burns the mouth of any animal that picks him up and so he is soon dropped in disgust !

Many legends and superstitions have grown up round the toad. Some say that he can live for many, many years sealed up in a cavity in rock. Others say he carries a jewel in his head ! Do you remember Jacques in " As You Like It " saying :

> *Sweet are the uses of adversity ;*
> *Which, like the toad, ugly and venomous,*
> *Wears yet a precious jewel in his head.*

And then witches were always supposed to use toads for their spells. But I like to think of the poor old toad as the famous

Mr. Toad in Kenneth Grahame's *The Wind in the Willows*, which I mentioned at the beginning of this chapter.

Another relation of the frog is the newt and you are likely to find some in most ponds in the spring. Newts—or efts—start their lives in the same way and pass through tadpole stages in the water. Unlike the other tadpoles, though, the newt keeps his tail for life and uses it for swimming. Our largest newt is called the crested newt and is more often seen on land than in the water. There is also a smaller relation called the smooth newt.

When the newt tadpole emerges from the egg—and the eggs are laid *separately* and then wrapped in the leaves of certain water weeds—he is almost entirely transparent. He develops more slowly than the frog and although he is quite harmless he protects himself in the same way as the toad with a bitter-tasting fluid given off by glands in the skin when he is frightened.

Frogs, toads and newts have plenty of enemies, but they do no harm and eat insects and harmful slugs—so do not kill them, please.

There are other forms of wild life in the pond, such as water insects and water spiders and snails and slugs, but there is not room to tell you about them here.

* * *

How to Build a Dam

To dam a stream is great fun, but you must be sure that in doing so you are not holding up or diverting water used downstream by a farmer. The best sort of water in which to play this game is a fast-running mountain stream with a rocky bed. Choose a place where the banks are narrow and fairly deep and the stream about three feet wide. Remember that there should be space *above* the dam for the water to collect so that the deeper the banks the deeper will be the pool that will form.

First collect some biggish rocks from the pool and lay them between the narrowest part of the banks on the bed of the stream. Build your dam from each *side* leaving a space in the middle for the water to rush through until you are ready to check it finally. Stones alone will not, of course, stop the flow of water, but they will act as a foundation. Clay is ideal to fill in the cracks and " cement " the loose stones, but if this is not available you will have to break away soil from the banks or, better still, cut large lumps of turf from nearby. Don't spoil the path in doing this, but cut from places where the gaps will not offend others coming the same way. Get the pieces of turf cut ready before you start building. You will get on much more quickly if there are two of you building from each bank at the same time.

Make your foundation very heavy, for water is very strong and will always find a weak place. When the rocks are in position place the turves firmly in front of them and as they become water-logged they will fit more easily into the cracks and crevices. Watch for weaknesses as the water rises. Gradually narrow the gap and then, when you have enough material ready, bang it down in the centre and work like mad to stop the flow. As the pressure on the dam increases have plenty more turves ready for an emergency. If the dam seems secure you can cut a channel or two for overflow streams from the rapidly filling pool or leave the water to find its own way over the top of the banks. If the dam holds firm you can loosen just one stone from the dry side and watch the weight of water break down the rest !

Books to Read

THE books I have listed here for you may not be in print when you read this, but any bookseller will tell you about them and get them for you—either new or secondhand—if he can. I have given the name of the publisher of every book, but not the price, because prices change so often. There are many more books dealing with the countryside and natural history than I give you here, but you will find a good selection in every public library. I hope these suggestions will help you to enjoy the countryside more, and our own dear countryside in particular.

THE FARM

" The Farmyard," by F. Fraser Darling.

" Farms and Fields," by C. S. and C. S. Orwin.

" The Care of Farm Animals," by F. Fraser Darling.

(These three books are published by the Oxford University Press and the National Federation of Young Farmers' Clubs.)

" The Seasons and the Farmer," by F. Fraser Darling (*Cambridge University Press*).

" Corduroy," " Silver Ley," and " The Cherry Tree " are three stories by Adrian Bell about his own farm (*John Lane The Bodley Head*).

Older children will enjoy these.

" I Bought a Mountain," by Thomas Firbank (*Harrap*).

This is another book not written specially for children, but it is the exciting, true story of a man who did actually buy a mountain in Wales and start sheep farming.

THE VILLAGE

" The Village," by F. G. Thomas (*Oxford University Press and the National Federation of Young Farmers' Clubs*).

" My Parish Church," by Basil F. L. Clarke (*Society for Promoting Christian Knowledge*).

" Village and Town," by S. R. Badmin (*Puffin Books*).

" The Village Carpenter," by Walter Rose (*Cambridge University Press*).

" A History of the Countryside," by Margaret and Alexander Potter (*Puffin Books*).

" A History of Everyday Things in England," by Marjorie and C. H. B. Quennell (*Batsford*).

This famous book in four volumes is an exciting and different sort of history of England.

ANIMALS OF THE COUNTRYSIDE

" Wild Animals of our Country," by W. S. Berridge (*Harrap*).

" Animals of the Countryside," by Arnid Johnston (*Puffin Books*).

" Diana my Badger," by Frances Pitt (*A. & C. Black*).

" Skewbald," by A. W. Seaby (*A. & C. Black*).
The story of a New Forest pony.

" The Open Book of Wild Life," by Richard Morse (*A. & C. Black*).

" Wild Life Through the Year," by Richard Morse (*A. & C. Black*).

These two books by Richard Morse tell you about all phases of wild life and not animals only.

" Reynard the Fox," by John Masefield (*Heinemann*).
This is an exciting story in verse form of a fox hunt.

" Tarka the Otter," by Henry Williamson (*Putnam*).
For older children.

" Owd Bob," by A. Olliphant (*Heinemann*).
The story of a sheepdog.

" Natural History of Selborne," by Gilbert White (*various publishers*).

" Moorland Mousie," by " Golden Gorse " (*Country Life*).
A favourite and delightful story of a horse.

" Black Beauty," by Anna Sewell (*various publishers*).
The classic life-story of a horse—first published seventy years ago and still popular.

" Five Proud Riders," by Ann Stafford (*Hamish Hamilton*).
Children and horses in the New Forest.

WOODS AND FORESTS

" The Seasons and the Woodman," by D. H. Chapman (*Cambridge University Press*).

" Trees," by Janet Harvey Kelman, described by C. E. Smith (*Nelson*).

" Trees in Britain," by S. R. Badmin (*Puffin Books*).

" A Pocket Book of British Trees," by E. H. B. Boulton (*A. & C. Black*).

BIRDS

" Birds," by M. K. C. Scott, described by J. A. Henderson (*Nelson*).

" The Charm of Birds," by Viscount Grey (*Hodder & Stoughton*).

If you love birds, you will enjoy this book, even though it was not specially written for children.

" Observer's Book of British Birds," by S. Vere Benson (*Warne*). *Three volumes.*

" A Book of Common Birds," by E. Sandars (*Oxford University Press*).

" A Pocket Book of British Birds," by Charles A. Hall (*A. & C. Black*).

" Birds of the Village," by James Fisher (*Puffin Books*).

" Bird Watching," by James Fisher (*Penguin Books*).

" A Bird Book for the Pocket," by E. Sandars (*Oxford University Press*).

FLOWERS

" A Flower Book for the Pocket," by Macgregor Skene (*Oxford University Press*).

" Wayside and Woodland Blossoms " (three volumes), by Edward Step (*Warne*).

" Botany for Children," by Lady Elphinstone (*Burns, Oates & Washbourne*).

" A Pocket Book of British Wild Flowers," by Charles A. Hall (*A. & C. Black*).

" Observer's Book of British Wild Flowers," by W. T. Stokoe (*Warne*).

Here are a few books—some of them story-books—with the English countryside as a background.

" Puck of Pook's Hill," by Rudyard Kipling (*Macmillan*).

A lovely book in which two children, guided and enchanted by Puck, meet with historical characters of the past.

" The Wind in the Willows," by Kenneth Grahame (*Methuen*).

" The Country Child," by Alison Uttley (*Faber*).

An unforgettable picture of life in an old farmhouse which most children will enjoy.

" I Know an Island," by R. M. Lockley (*Harrap*).

Stories of wild life and bird-watching on several small islands round our coasts. Thrilling and true. For older children.

" Lorna Doone," by R. D. Blackmore (*various publishers and editions*).

A thrilling story set in wild Exmoor in the time of Judge Jeffreys.

" Children of the New Forest," by F. Marryat (*various publishers*).

The story of how a Royalist family, forced to leave their home, took refuge in the New Forest.

" Bevis," by Richard Jefferies (*various publishers*).

A classic story of a boy and his adventures in the country.

BRITISH HERITAGE AND COUNTRYSIDE

Although not written for children, there are two splendid series of books published by Batsford. *The British Heritage* series deals with Castles, Churches, Cathedrals, Villages and Country Customs, while the *Face of Britain* books survey, in picture and story, different districts of Britain.

RIVERS, PONDS AND STREAMS

" The Seasons and the Fisherman," by F. Fraser Darling (*Cambridge University Press*).

" The Fishes of the British Isles," by J. Travis Jenkins (*Warne*).

" The Observer's Book of Freshwater Fishes of the British Isles," by A. Laurence Wells (*Warne*).

" How to see Pond Life," by E. F. Daglish (*Dent*).

PUCK'S SONG

See you the dimpled track that runs,
　All hollow through the wheat ?
O that was where they hauled the guns
　That smote King Philip's fleet.

See you our little mill that clacks,
　So busy by the brook ?
She has ground her corn and paid her tax
　Ever since Domesday book.

See you our stilly woods of oak,
　And the dread ditch beside ?
O that was where the Saxons broke,
　On the day that Harold died.

See you the windy levels spread
　About the gates of Rye ?
O that was where the Northmen fled,
　When Alfred's ships came by.

See you our pastures wide and lone,
　Where the red oxen browse ?
O there was a city thronged and known,
　Ere London boasted a house.

And see you, after rain, the trace
　Of mound and ditch and wall ?
O that was a Legion's camping-place,
　When Cæsar sailed from Gaul.

And see you the marks that show and fade,
　Like shadows on the Downs ?
O they are the lines the Flint Men made,
　To guard their wondrous towns.

Trackway and Camp and City lost,
　Salt Marsh where now is corn ;
Old Wars, old Peace, old Arts that cease,
　And so was England born !

She is not any common Earth,
　Water or wood or air,
But Merlin's Isle of Gramarye,
　Where you and I will fare.

RUDYARD KIPLING

INDEX

INDEX

Made and Printed in Great Britain by
Hazell, Watson & Viney Ltd. London and Aylesbury

7/6